Gerard Manley Hopkins

A Study of Selected Poems

Gerard Manley Hopkins:
A study of Selected Poems

John Gilroy

HEB ☼ Humanities-Ebooks

Published by *Humanities-Ebooks.co.uk*
Tirril Hall, Tirril, Penrith CA10 2JE

ISBN 978-1-84760-012-7 PDF
ISBN 978-1-84760-367-8 Paperback

In memory of
Mgr K.F.Nichols (1929–2006)
Poet and teacher

Contents

Acknowledgments

The author wishes to thank: Charles Moseley for valuable editorial advice; The National Portrait Gallery, London, for permission to reproduce the two portraits of Hopkins; and the Tate Gallery, Millbank, London for permission to reproduce the picture, 'Snowstorm – Steam Boat off a Harbour's Mouth' by J. M. W. Turner. Work in copyright is reproduced by permission of Oxford University Press on behalf of the British Province of the Society of Jesus.

Cover Illustration:
'Manley Hopkins' by Forshaw and Coles (1880)
National Portrait Gallery, London

Part 1. Life and Times

1.1 Early life and Schooldays

Gerard Manley Hopkins was born in 1844 at Stratford in Essex, the eldest of nine children, several of whom were talented. Two of his brothers, Arthur and Everard grew up to be artists and illustrators for prominent publications such as *Punch* and the *Illustrated London News*. A brother, Lionel, became a Consul in China and an expert on the Chinese language, while a sister, Grace, had skills as a musician and composer. The children's father, Manley Hopkins, acted as Consul-General for Hawaii, pursued a profession as a marine insurance adjuster and was, by degrees, mathematician, poet, novelist and reviewer. His wife, Kate, was well-educated with literary and musical tastes and a competence in languages, and his sister, Ann ('Aunt Annie'), a talented painter, produced the portrait of G. M. Hopkins at the age of fourteen which is now in the National Portrait Gallery, London. In Gerard, it seems, all these various accomplishments in language, in literature, art and music came together to produce in the course of time the unique corpus of poetry that would make him famous.

The Hopkins family was solidly middle-class and Anglican in religion. From childhood, Gerard shared their devoutness which deepened as he matured, leading finally to his conversion to Catholicism and ordination into the Roman Catholic priesthood. When he was eight years old the family moved from Stratford to fashionable Hampstead in North London and he was sent to Highgate School. There he became friendly with, among others, Marcus Clarke who wrote the novel, *For the Term of His Natural*

'Gerard Manley Hopkins'
by Anne Eleanor Hopkins (1859)
National Portrait Gallery, London

Life (1870), and Ernest Coleridge, grandson of the poet who had lived, died and was buried at Highgate. Perhaps Coleridge's most famous poem, 'The Rime of the Ancyent Marinere', had something to do with the much-quoted schooldays episode of Hopkins's abstinence (ostensibly for a bet) from all liquids for three weeks. 'The real reason', wrote a schoolfriend, Charles Luxmoore, was 'a conversation on seamen's sufferings and human powers of endurance' (FL 395). 'With throats unslaked, with black lips baked' (l.162) is certainly similar to a schoolfellow's recollection of 'Gerard showing him his tongue just before the end and it was black' (FL 395). Manley Hopkins, in his youth, had written a poem, 'The Philosopher's Stone', in the manner of the 'Ancyent Marinere', and two of Hopkins's poems from his schooldays, 'Spring and Death', and 'Winter with the Gulf Stream' contain phrases on which Coleridge's poem has obviously been something of an influence. In any event, the story points to an early strength of will and the kind of rigorous determination which would characterise the poet for the rest of his life.

Hopkins's years at Highgate were academically distinguished and he proved to be a brilliant classical scholar as well as a potentially talented poet, winning school prize for a composition entitled 'The Escorial' in 1860. The poem, in Spenserian stanzas,[1] with its echoes of Keats and its interest in architecture, and another early illustrated poem, 'A Vision of the Mermaids' with 'Winter with the Gulf Stream' in the notoriously difficult terza rima form[2] bring together, at this comparatively early stage, many of the mature poet's characteristics, the visual, sensual and formalist elements associated with his later work.

1.2 Oxford

In April 1863 Hopkins went on a scholarship to Balliol College, Oxford, to study Classics. One of his tutors, Benjamin Jowett, University Professor of Greek and later the Master of Balliol, was leader of the Broad Church movement there. The Broad Church faction at Oxford University, at this time an ecclesiastical institution run exclusively by dons who were celibate and in orders, was attempting to reconcile the fundamental truths of Christian belief with the increasingly invasive rationalism of the nineteenth century. In his collection entitled *Essays and Reviews* (1860), Jowett had caused a furore among the authorities for what were considered to be hetero-

---

1 A stanza form used by Edmund Spenser for *The Faerie Queene* (1590-96) in which the first eight 8 lines are in iambic pentameter and the ninth is an iambic hexameter (an Alexandrine).

2 Interlinked tercets where each is joined to the one following by a common rhyme: aba, bcb, cdc, and so on.

dox notions inimical to the very basis of Christianity. Broad Church adherents were somewhere between the two other branches of belief within the University during Hopkins's time. At one end of the spectrum were the Evangelicals, subscribing to a literal interpretation of biblical revelation and firmly within the Protestant tradition. At the other was the High Church party, associated particularly with E. B. Pusey, the Professor of Hebrew, and Canon H. P. Liddon of Christ Church. The High Church in principle was essentially Catholic, but purist, avoiding what it saw as the errors of Protestantism and Catholicism alike. Espousing ritualism, it shared many Catholic beliefs, the fundamental exception being the Church's teaching on the Real Presence of the body and blood of Christ in Holy Communion. Pusey had originally been part of the Oxford Movement during the 1830's, an attempt, through a series of publications called *Tracts for the Times*, to throw back the advance of atheistic rationalism by stressing the importance of established beliefs and traditional modes of worship. Prominent among the Tractarians, as they were known, was John Henry Newman whose famous 'Tract XC' had been an important milestone on his progress along the road to full communion with the Catholic Church and to which he in fact converted (with many of his followers) in 1845. He became a Catholic priest in the following year, and in 1847 founded the Oratory School at Birmingham where Hopkins would teach for a short time after he was received into the Church by Newman in 1866. In the meanwhile, however, he was, at Oxford, an avowed High Churchman associating with groups of like-minded undergraduates within the orbits of Pusey and of Liddon who became his confessor. His aesthetic side obviously responded to High Church ritualism, yet when he did eventually go over to Rome he was especially anxious to stress to his devastated father that the aesthetic dimension of Catholicism had played no part in his decision: 'I am surprised you shd. say fancy and aesthetic taste have led me to my present state of mind: these wd. be better satisfied in the Church of England, for bad taste is always meeting one in the accessories of Catholicism' (FL 93).

Apart from his academic programme and theological preoccupations, Hopkins had time to enjoy other aspects of being a university student, and it was in these years that he made the acquaintance of and friendships with tutors and peers who would become influential in his comparatively short future life. Apart from Jowett, himself, also to be mentioned are Walter Pater, who was a leading figure in the later nineteenth century Aesthetic ('Art for Art's sake') movement, and T. H. Green, his tutor in philosophy. Undoubtedly the single most important friendship that Hopkins made was with his fellow student, Robert Bridges, the later Poet Laureate and first editor of a collected edition of his poems in 1918. Their relationship was always slightly coloured, however, by the fact that Bridges did not share, and was somewhat irritated by, his friend's beliefs and eventual vocation. By profession he was a doctor and, like Keats before him, would later abandon medicine for poetry. Along with Canon Dixon, a some time teacher of Hopkins at Highgate, and Coventry Patmore, the celebrated Victorian poet and author of 'The Angel in the House', whom Hopkins met later in life, Bridges was virtually the only reader of Hopkins's poetry during the poet's lifetime. His *Editor's Preface* in 1918 was not uncritical of his friend's work but, nevertheless, without his careful custodianship of the legacy, Hopkins's poems might never have been known at all. Bridges's very touching sonnet to him is to be found placed before Hopkins's own *Author's Preface* in the first edition.

As an undergraduate Hopkins wrote many poems in a variety of styles. These are the verses to which he was probably referring in his Journal entry for 11 May 1868, 'Slaughter of the Innocents' (J 165), and of which he speaks ten years later to Canon Dixon:

> What I had written I burnt before I became a Jesuit and resolved to write no more, as not belonging to my profession unless it were by the wish of my superiors; so for seven years I wrote nothing but two or three little presentation pieces which occasion called for (LD 14).

The details underlying this important episode are discussed in *The Journals and Papers of Gerard Manley Hopkins* pp.165 and 538. The seven years to which Hopkins refers obviously represented for him a period of remarkable development between the slightly mannered and derivative verse of his early creative period, and his extraordinary achievement in 'The Wreck of the Deutschland', the poem with which he broke his poetic silence in 1875. By this time, of course, he was a member of the Jesuit order and regarded poetry as a merely tangential activity to what he now considered to be the sole purpose of his life. The Oxford years, however, established much that was carried into his later creativity and the early diaries and journals are a fruitful resource for the critical examination of the major work. One significant influence on Hopkins's detailed visual perception was John Ruskin, soon to be appointed to the Chair of Art at Oxford, and it is clear that the accounts of natural phenomena which permeate Hopkins's early writings, as well as his accomplished drawings of the natural world and of architecture,[1] owe their accuracy to the close attention to detail associated with Ruskin in works such as *Modern Painters* (1843-60).

A writer who had also read *Modern Painters* and to whom Hopkins bears some

---

1   See plates between pp. 455 and 456 of *The Journal and Papers of Gerard Manley Hopkins*

striking resemblance is the American naturalist, Henry David Thoreau (1817–62), and it is worth considering Thoreau for a moment in this connection. In his Journal Thoreau expressed some disappointment at not finding in *Modern Painters*, 'a more out-of-door book'. Ruskin does not describe Nature as Nature, he writes, 'but as Turner has painted her, and though the work betrays that he has given a close attention to Nature, it appears to have been with an artist's and critic's design' (Thoreau, Journal.X.69, Oct. 6 1857)[1]. With his own 'out-of-door' observations of the feathers of frostwork on panes of glass Thoreau writes: 'I was never so struck by the gracefulness of the curves in vegetation, and wonder that Ruskin does not refer to frostwork' (Thoreau, Journal.X.209, Nov. 27 1857). Hopkins's own visual sense, like Thoreau's, could often be very individual, even surprising, in expression, and one might imagine, therefore, Thoreau being sympathetic with a journal entry such as the following, written during the second year of Hopkins's Jesuit novitiate at Roehampton when part of his duties involved washing out the urinals there: 'The slate slabs of the urinals even are frosted in graceful sprays' (J 196); or with his description of the Giessbach Falls with 'curled edges [...] like the crispiest endive' (J 173), or mountain snow 'cut off short as crisp as celery' (J 174). The latter two entries made during his journey in Switzerland in 1868 are typical of the individuality of Hopkins's perceptions for which he constantly needed space and solitude. 'Even with one companion', he writes, [he was travelling with a friend, Edward Bond] 'ecstasy is almost banished: you want to be alone and to feel that, and leisure – all pressure taken off' (J 182). Similarly, Thoreau: 'I thrive best on solitude. If I have had a companion only one day in a week [...] I find that the value of the week to me has been seriously affected' (Thoreau, Journal.IX.200, Dec.28 1856).

Some details are very close indeed, as in the following examples. In the 'Spring' chapter of *Walden* (1854) Thoreau makes an organic metaphor out of the movement and shapes of earth and sand which he notices in a cutting:

> Few phenomena gave me more delight than to observe the forms which thawing sand and clay assume in flowing down the sides of a deep cut [...] Innumerable little streams overlap and interlace one with another, exhibiting a sort of hybrid product, which obeys half way the law of currents, and half way that of vegetation'.

Compare Hopkins's Journal entry:

---

1   Bradford Torrey and Francis H. Allen eds. *The Journal of Henry D. Thoreau*, 2 Vols (New York: Dover Publications, 1962)

I think it was the same day I saw where rainwater had run through one of the cuttings made to carry it off in the turf by the side of the road, and the gully being sandy, it had carried the sand down into the road, throwing it in clear expression into a branched root or, if you looked at it from above downwards, a "treated" tree head' (J 157).

The thawing sand and clay leads Thoreau to some linguistic speculations, very similar to those which Hopkins deploys throughout his early diaries:

No wonder that the earth expresses itself outwardly in leaves, it so labours with the idea inwardly [...] The overhanging leaf sees here its prototype. *Internally*, whether in the globe or animal body, it is a moist thick *lobe* [...] (...*labor*, *lapsus*, to flow or slip downward, [...] *globus*, lobe, globe; also lap,flap, and many other words); *externally*, a dry thin *leaf*, even as the *f* and *v* are a pressed and dried *b*. The radicals of *lobe* are *lb*, the soft mass of the *b* (single-lobed, or B, double-lobed), with the liquid *l* behind it pressing it forward. In globe, *glb*, the guttural *g* adds to the meaning the capacity of the throat.

Here is a typical Hopkins diary entry of 1863:

'*Flag*, (droop etc), flaccere, notion that of waving instead of rigidity, flowing (as we say of drapery). Hence *flag* the substantive. *Fledge* to furnish with wings with which to compare *fly*, *fled*, etc above. With fillip, flip cf. flap, flob. Cf. the connection between *flag* and *flabby* with that between *flick* and *flip*, *flog*, and *flap*, *flop* (J 11–12).

In *Walden* Thoreau scrutinizes the frozen pond in winter:

I look down into the quiet parlor of the fishes, pervaded by a softened light as through a window of ground glass, with its bright sanded floor the same as in summer; there a perennial waveless serenity reigns as in the amber twilight sky, corresponding to the cool and even temperament of the inhabitants. Heaven is under our feet as well as over our heads (Ch.16)

A journal entry finds Hopkins at Stonyhurst College in 1870 similarly employed:

Looking down into the thick ice of our pond I found the imprisoned air-bubbles nothing at random but starting from centres and in particular one most beautifully regular white brush of them, each spur of it a curving string of beaded and diminishing bubbles (J 201–2).

This emphasis on the steady observing eye was something that Ruskin, Thoreau and Hopkins inherited from the Romantics. Wordsworth, for example, often makes use of phrases such as, 'I looked and looked', 'I gazed and gazed', 'I stopped and stared'. 'At all times', he said, 'I have [...] endeavoured to look steadily at my subject'.[1] A sense of reciprocity between the observing poet and the natural world stems from this close attention. 'What you look hard at', writes Hopkins, 'seems to look hard at you' (J 204), a statement anticipated by one of his favourite poets, Keats:

> Hyperion arose, and on the stars
> Lifted his curved lids, and kept them wide
> Until it ceased; and still he kept them wide;
> And still they were the same bright, patient stars[2]

What was important for Hopkins, however, and equally important for Wordsworth, Ruskin and Thoreau, was the spiritual and moral value attaching to such close observation. To see nature accurately was also to be made good by it, to achieve a moral perception.

1.3 Conversion to Catholicism

The most momentous episode for Hopkins during his time at Oxford was undoubtedly his conversion from the Anglican faith to Catholicism. This was a decision he had reached by the autumn of 1866. The period leading up to it from 1865, however, is very much bound up in the story of his encounter with a seventeen year old youth, and a distant relative of Bridges, named Digby Dolben. A former pupil at Eton College, Dolben was a High Church Anglican with strong Catholic leanings and also a burgeoning poet of somewhat highly wrought, emotional religious verse. He intended eventually to enter Balliol College and, with this in mind, visited Oxford in February 1865 where he met Hopkins. Although there was never another meeting between them it is clear that, on Hopkins's part at least, a deeply spiritual as well as an emotional and physical attraction ensued. Victorian society certainly countenanced the kind of male homosocial relationships which are perhaps now, in our own century, in danger of being misconstrued. But while there is no surviving evidence of anything specifically homosexual in Hopkins's behaviour with Dolben, the episode does point

---

1   Preface to *Lyrical Ballads* 1800. This Preface which is now regarded as an integral part of the collection did not appear in the first edition of 1798
2   *Hyperion*, 1, ll.350–3

up the extent to which the physical and spiritual are closely integrated within his personality. Dolben's religiosity was a predominant part of his appeal to Hopkins and at a particularly sensitive time for him when he was contemplating a radical change in his spiritual life. There is, indeed, plenty of evidence throughout the poetry and writings of an aesthetic appreciation of physical beauty, and very often male physical beauty as in, for example, 'Harry Ploughman', or in 'To What Serves Mortal Beauty?' where, in the latter, 'mortal beauty' is described as 'dangerous'. In a letter of 1868 to his friend, Alexander Baillie, Hopkins acknowledged this 'danger' when remembering how, earlier in his life, he had wanted to be a painter: 'But even if I could I wd. not I think now', he wrote, 'for the fact is that the higher and more attractive parts of the art put a strain upon the passions which I shd. think it unsafe to encounter' (FL 231). When all is said and done, this one obvious and deeply emotional affection for Dolben was perhaps only to be expected at a time in Hopkins's very early manhood, and when male bonding in what was almost exclusively a male-dominated Oxford society was the norm rather than the exception. As things turned out, Dolben's life ended tragically in a drowning accident in 1867, by which time Hopkins was able to write to Bridges with a certain amount of detachment about him:

> I find it difficult to realise his death or feel as if it were anything to me. You know there can very seldom have happened the loss of so much beauty (in body and mind and life) [...] seldom I mean, in the whole world, for the conditions wd. not easily come together (LB 16–17).

Meanwhile, Hopkins's resolve to become a Catholic was strengthening. On a walking holiday with his friend, William Addis, in the summer of 1866, he met Canon Paul Raynal at the Benedictine monastery at Belmont in Herefordshire. According to Addis, Canon Raynal made a firm impression on both of them, and just over a month later, on 17 July, Hopkins wrote in his journal, 'It was this night I believe but possibly the next that I saw clearly the impossibility of staying in the Church of England' (J 146). In September, having approached him by letter for advice, Hopkins met with Newman whose famous *Apologia Pro Vita Sua*, describing his own path to Rome, had been published two years previously. To the dismay of Dr Pusey, and of Canon Liddon who tried desperately, at Manley Hopkins's request, to get Hopkins to change his mind, he was received into the Roman Catholic Church by Newman at the Birmingham Oratory on 21 October, 1866.

The most devastating effect was on his parents. That a much loved son had abandoned their Church without any apparent feelings for them, or consideration, as they thought, for what he was really doing, produced a painful exchange of letters. (FL 91–100). Catholicism in England at this time was only gradually emerging from centuries of persecution and suspicion and, until the period when Hopkins was a student at Balliol, colleges had made it obligatory for undergraduates to be members of the Anglican community. Not only did Hopkins's degree seem imperilled by his decision, but also the whole of his future life and expectations seemed likely to be compromised by his conversion. As it turned out, however, Balliol College removed its penalisation of Catholic undergraduates and Newman encouraged Hopkins to sit for his degree, even though the official position of the Church was to deny Catholics attendance at the ancient universities, suspecting Oxford and Cambridge of being potentially heretical environments. Far from thoughtlessly converting as his father had implied, however, it was clear from one of Hopkins's letters to him that the process had been thoroughly considered:

> My conversion is due to the following reasons mainly [...] (i) simple and strictly drawn arguments partly my own, partly others', (ii) common sense, (iii) reading the Bible, especially the Holy Gospels, where texts like "Thou art Peter" (the evasions proposed for this alone are enough to make one a Catholic) [...]so pursued me that at one time I thought it best to stop thinking of them, (iv) an increasing knowledge of the Catholic system [...] which only wants to be known in order to be loved – its consolations, its marvellous ideal of holiness, the faith and devotion of its children, its multiplicity, its array of saints and martyrs, its consistency and unity, its glowing prayers, the daring majesty of its claims, etc etc (FL 93).

With Hopkins securely within the fold of the Church of Rome relations with his parents gradually improved, he gained a first-class degree and, after a brief excursion to Paris with a friend, took up a teaching post at Newman's Oratory School in Birmingham. Teaching for him was never a congenial occupation, even though his future career would require him to undertake it on a fairly regular basis, and a retreat at the Oratory in Holy Week, 1868, given by the Jesuit Father Henry Coleridge, seems to have been crucial in his decision some weeks later to apply for acceptance into the Jesuit order as a priest of the Roman Catholic Church.

1.4 Hopkins the Jesuit

If Catholicism was still regarded as a 'foreign' religion, the Jesuit order, founded

Manley Hopkins by Forshaw and Coles (1880)
National Portrait Gallery, London

in the mid-sixteenth century as a spearhead of the Counter-Reformation, was regarded by many as its secret society. From their beginnings the Jesuits have been the intellectual arm of the Catholic Church and their lives as teachers and missionaries organised with military discipline. When his decision had been made, Hopkins wrote to his one time confessor, Canon Liddon: 'After a few weeks' tour in Switzerland which I am hoping to make I am going to enter the Jesuit noviciate at Roehampton: I do not think there is another prospect so bright in the world' (FL 49). Five years later his mind has not changed; to Baillie he writes: 'this life here [at Stonyhurst, Lancs.] though it is hard is God's will for me as I most intimately know, which is more than violets knee-deep' (FL 235).

In his Swiss tour of July 1868, Hopkins was accompanied by an Oxford friend, Edward Bond and, though it was of shorter duration, the expedition is in many ways reminiscent of the walking tour of the Alps made by Wordsworth and Robert Jones in the summer of 1790. Hopkins's detailed accounts, his descriptions of waterfalls 'shooting in races' with droplets 'blown upwards by the blast of the vapour as it rises' (J 177) are close to Wordsworth's 'torrents shooting from the clear blue sky' and 'stationary blasts of waterfalls',[1] and often his observations prefigure in their descriptions the kind of lines to be encountered in his own later poems. The reason for the tour in the first place was Bond telling Hopkins that the Jesuits '[were] strictly forbidden the country' (FL 53). This was, therefore, his last opportunity to travel freely in a landscape which had been inspirational to so many writers including, more recently, and significantly for Hopkins, John Ruskin. To read through the journal entries with their delighted sense of freedom, descriptions of large vistas and impassioned perceptual detail is also to discover gradually the sense of confinement, the narrowing of horizons, in the literal sense, of Hopkins's world when, just over a year later, one comes across the following kind of remark with a very 'indoors' feeling: 'A few days before

---

1   *The Prelude*, 1805, VI, ll. 561-558

Sept.25 a fine sunrise seen from no.1, the upstairs bedroom' or again: 'About the same time a fine sunset [...] looked at also from the upstairs windows' (J 192). These notes are a reminder that, henceforward, Hopkins's movements would inevitably be restricted by the demands of the order to which he had now committed his life.

The routine of a Jesuit is based upon the Spiritual Exercises of his community's founder, St Ignatius Loyola. They are a methodical and logical sequence of meditations encouraging repentance, reformation and a desire to imitate Christ to the exclusion of everything else in this life. The opening sentences of the 'First Principle and Foundation', therefore, must be understood as the very basis of Hopkins's daily existence and the *sine qua non* for readers, it has to be said, for any real understanding of what he saw as the true purpose behind his life and work. They read:

> Man was created to praise, reverence and serve God Our Lord, and by so doing to save his soul. And the other things on the face of the earth were created for man's sake and to help him in the carrying out of the end for which he was created (SD 122)

When he embarked as a 'scholastic' on the lengthy Jesuit training, Hopkins was moved among the various houses of the order. After his two year 'Novitiate' at Manresa House, Roehampton, near London, he went on to Stonyhurst College in Lancashire for a three year period of study in mathematics and philosophy (the 'Philosophate'). He then returned to Roehampton for a year to teach 'Rhetoric' before entering his final phase at the Jesuit house, St Bueno's, in North Wales. Here he spent his three year 'Theologate', a rigorous study of moral theology – in all, an exacting nine years of training leading to ordination in 1877. Although each of these periods had its significant role to play in his development, by far the most important for his achievement in poetry was the time that he spent in the beautiful Welsh rural surroundings of St Bueno's. Here, at a hint from its Rector, Fr Jones, he wrote his masterpiece, 'The Wreck of the Deutschland', an occasional poem about a shipwreck in 1875 at the mouth of the Thames. And although his attempt to publish it with the Jesuit *Month* was rebuffed (as was later 'The Loss of the Eurydice' in 1878) and led to his abandonment of any further publishing ambitions, Hopkins now felt that at least he was no longer under restraint from his order and was free to write poetry if he wished to do so.

His new voice, an extraordinary and innovative blend of intensity and technique, is at once evident in the 'core' poems he wrote at St Bueno's in 1877, among which are many of those for which he is now best known: 'Spring', 'The Windhover',

'The Starlight Night', 'God's Grandeur', 'The Lantern Out of Doors', 'Hurrahing in Harvest' and 'Pied Beauty' – all of them wonderfully expressive achievements, full of a joyful celebration of the natural world and a profound reverence for the God he describes as being 'under the world's splendour and wonder'.[1]

Throughout his ministry a Jesuit priest expects to be moved from place to place. In the seven years that followed his ordination Hopkins was variously Sub-minister in Chesterfield, Select Preacher at Farm Street Church in Mayfair, London, and a priest at Oxford, Bedford Leigh, Manchester, Liverpool and Glasgow, as well as being teacher of classics at Stonyhurst. During this whole period he continued to write poetry, but the sheer number of placements suggests that the order was clearly finding it difficult to establish someone as idiosyncratic as Hopkins in a situation suitable to his particular talents. The time spent in the industrial North was the most trying for his temperament. His references in letters to mills and coal pits, the stench of sulphuretted hydrogen rolling in the air and forming on railing and pavement (LB 90), his 'sorrow and loathing' at 'the base and bespotted figures and features of the Liverpool crowd' (LB 127) and his 'unbearable thought that by degrees almost all our population will become a town population and a puny unhealthy and cowardly one' (FL 293) reflect a particularly Victorian anxiety shared by figures such as Dickens in *Hard Times* (1854) and 'Condition of England' writers like Thomas Carlyle, Mrs Gaskell and John Ruskin. Even amidst the 'grey beauty' of Oxford Hopkins would notice the 'base and brickish skirt' of the industrial suburbs steadily encroaching on the 'rural keeping' of the ancient city ('Duns Scotus's Oxford').

Eventually, the Jesuits despatched him to Ireland where, in February 1884, he took up the post of Professor of Greek at the Catholic University College in Dublin. The last five years of his life, divided between teaching (a colleague was Thomas Arnold, brother of Matthew Arnold and Professor of English) and an overwhelming commitment to the marking of hundreds of examination papers drawn from all over the country several times a year, inexorably wore down his stamina. 'It is killing work to examine a nation', he wrote to Dixon (LD 154). He had always suffered from variable degrees of physical frailty but now, added to it, was a psychological condition arising, it seems, from a number of causes. One was his personal situation made difficult by friction between his deeply patriotic sentiments and his attitude to the Irish Home Rule movement. Hopkins, as a Catholic, found himself, at odds with the Irish Protestants, but his opposition to nationalism made him an unsympathetic figure in Catholic eyes. Added to this dilemma, and no doubt exacerbated by his chronic

---

1   'The Wreck of the *Deutschland'* st. 5

nervous exhaustion, was a pervasive sense that having given up so much by his conversion and then, shortly afterwards, his vocation, he had been abandoned by the God in whom he continued so fervently to believe. The mental agonies he suffered, fortunately for posterity, found expression in six great sonnets of desolation, most of them written in 1885: 'I wake and feel the fell of dark, not day', 'No worst, there is none', ('Carrion Comfort'),[1] 'Patience, hard thing!', 'My own heart let me more have pity on' and 'Thou art indeed just, Lord, if I contend'. These sonnets, more conventional in form than his other experimental ones, are among the greatest devotional verses in the language. They are the culmination of the fourteen years of Hopkins's mature output, in all amounting to fewer than fifty poems but all of which are now regarded as of major importance, and most of them almost completely unknown until practically thirty years after his death.

Hopkins is very much a man of his age in aspects of his cultural nationalism and, amongst other things, in the associations he can be shown to have with prominent nineteenth century contemporaries such as Tennyson, Browning, Swinburne and Christina Rossetti. On the other hand, his extraordinarily original poetry in terms of its semantics, formalism, prosody, symbolism, syntax and textual structuralism anticipates later developments, and it was therefore the more surprising for his first twentieth century readers to discover that by 1918 the poet had been dead for almost thirty years. The difficulty of where exactly to 'place' Hopkins has always been at the heart of critical debate about him.

After a short illness Hopkins died, at the age of forty-four, of typhoid fever on 8 June 1889. He was buried in the Jesuit plot of Glasnevin cemetery, Dublin, where only his name, with those of other members of his order, is to be found recorded on a monument there. Since the first collected edition of his poetry was published, Hopkins's reputation has continued to grow. Seldom, if ever, has a comparatively small body of work met with such wide acclaim, or a poet with a devotion to 'contempt of the world' been so honoured and celebrated by it.

---

1   Not Hopkins's title

Part 2. Strategies

2.1 Introduction

Hopkins was a classical scholar and to read his journals and letters is to recognise it at once in the ease and competence with which he handles complex matters of verse structure, metrical form and scansion. His 'ear' for rhythm is very accurate. In this example he is assessing a poem by his friend and correspondent, Canon Dixon, in which he hears literary echoes: '"Rattled her keys, unfavourable sign, /And on her turning wheel gan to decline". The first line is like "The Rape of the Lock": "Spadillio first, unconquerable lord" – the second like Spencer [sic]' (LD 83). Two of his primary interests, music and architecture, he describes as 'the only two arts that have any science to speak of' (LB 249) and he recognises 'a world of profound mathematics in this matter of music': (LD 135). As might be expected he applies a rigorous critical logic to the written word:

> I will give a glaring instance from Browning of false perspective in an image. In his *Instans Tyrannus* he makes the tyrant say that he found the just man his victim on a sudden shielded from him by the vault of the sky spreading itself like a great targe over him, "with the sun's disc for visible boss." This is monstrous. The vault of heaven is a vault, hollow, concave towards us, convex upwards; it therefore could only defend man on earth against enemies above it, an angry Olympus for instance. And the tyrant himself is inside it, under it, just as much as his victim. The boss is seen from behind, like the small stud of a sleevelink. This comes of frigid fancy with no imagination (LD 56-7)

Hopkins's own poems defy such criticism with their combination of feeling, observational accuracy and a powerful imagination. They are remarkable not so much for the things they are written about as for the unique way in which these things are given expression. In fact Hopkins is like no other poet. His voice, as C.Day Lewis remarked, 'seems to come out of the blue, reminding us of nothing we have heard before'.[1] His influence becomes immediately obvious when his techniques –'dangerous toys', as F. R. Leavis describes them[2] – are used by other poets.

Hopkins could be unsparing in his criticisms, and although tactful and sensitive to the feelings of others, he always maintains his ground. 'Perhaps I misunderstand the passage: I hope I do', he writes to Patmore, 'but then I hope you will prevent other people misunderstanding it' (FL 310). To Patmore again: 'I must surely have missed the clew to the meaning, for all this is far from the great felicity your figures have. I suppose I have, but then I think others will mostly miss it too' (FL 315). The criticisms were almost invariably accepted and his amendments implemented. In fact a small remark on one occasion caused Patmore to destroy a work on which he had spent ten years of his life, so much value was placed on Hopkins's judgement. Hopkins was himself acutely aware of his own original style and, like Keats whom he admired, was conscious of his status in relation to that of his contemporaries. 'So few people have style', he wrote, '[...] not Tennyson nor Swinburne nor Morris, not to name the misbegotten Browning crew' (LB 111). Browning, whose lack of imagination he criticized (above) had a way of talking, he once said, with 'the air and spirit of a man bouncing up from the table with his mouth full of bread and cheese and saying that he meant to stand no blasted nonsense' (LD 74). The poems of an equally distinguished contemporary, Matthew Arnold, he could describe as having 'all the ingredients of poetry without quite being it' (FL 58). Hopkins's own style emerges from something evident in his temperament from the beginning, the kind of rebelliousness or principled stubbornness reflected in one of his remarks to Bridges: 'The effect of studying masterpieces is to make me admire and do otherwise. So it must be on every original artist to some degree, on me to a marked degree' (LB 291). He wrote of his work as follows in a letter to Bridges in 1879:

> No doubt my poetry errs on the side of oddness [...] But as air, melody, is what strikes me most of all in music and design in painting, so design, pattern or what I am in the habit of calling 'inscape' is what I above all aim at in poetry. Now it is the virtue of design, pattern, or inscape to be distinctive and it is the vice of distinctiveness to become queer. This vice I cannot have escaped' (LB 66).

---

1   C. Day Lewis, *A Hope for Poetry* (Oxford: Basil Blackwell, 1934), p.74
2   F. R. Leavis, *New Bearings in English Poetry: A Study of the Contemporary Situation* (London: Chatto & Windus, 1932), p.193

2.2 Inscape

The term 'inscape', Hopkins's invention, is used both as noun: 'All the world is full of inscape and chance left free to act falls into an order as well as purpose:' (J 230) – and as verb: 'I looked at the groin or the flank and saw how the set of hair symmetrically flowed outwards from it to all parts of the body, so that, following that one may inscape the whole beast very simply' (J 242).

The word itself invites comparison with other 'scape' forms such as 'landscape' or 'seascape', which take the eye outwards to a wide prospect. The 'in' prefix of Hopkins's coinage directs the sight at something intrinsic to an object pressing out from within, and giving to that particular form its individual and literal 'ex-pression' or pattern. Hopkins had always been interested in the detail of the phenomenal world and considered it a fortunate event to have encountered the work of the medieval philosopher, Duns Scotus (1266-1308), during a period of residence at Stonyhurst in 1872. He describes in his journal of being at this time 'flush with a new stroke of enthusiasm' and writes: 'when I took in any inscape of the sky or sea I thought of Scotus' (J 221). Hopkins's enthusiasm stemmed from his belief that, in the eyes of his Jesuit superiors, Scotus's philosophy would sanction his own passionate response to the individual forms of natural phenomena. Catholic doctrine was essentially based on the 'Thomist' (St Thomas Aquinas) belief that God, as an abstract Being, could only be 'known' through generalities and not through the individualities of particular created things. Scotus, however, had maintained that each thing has its own distinctive essence or 'thisness' (the latin word he uses is 'haecceitas') which makes up its true reality – that God's own reality is an embodiment of these separate individuated forms which in themselves enable us to understand him. Hopkins found such notions sympathetic and two of his poems in particular, 'Pied Beauty' and 'Duns Scotus's Oxford', reflect this 'Scotian' vision of the world. The inscaping of 'each mortal thing', therefore, far from being for him a transgressive activity, actually sanctioned his deepest beliefs and ensured that his role as a Jesuit priest and his insights and strategies as poet were not, as he had feared, irreconcilable.

Hopkins was led to some amazing and idiosyncratic observations in which he was always trying to 'law out' the inscapes of things. 'I have now found the law of the oak leaves', he writes (J 146), or: 'Those tretted mossy clouds have their law more in helices, wave-tongues, than in anything else' (J 142). It would not be difficult to multiply examples from the journal in which an articulate liveliness and prose rhythm make some entries practically poems in themselves. The following is typical:

Today the river was wild, very full, glossy brown with mud, furrowed in permanent billows through which from head to head the water swung with a great down and up again. These heads were scalped with rags of jumping foam. But at the Roughs the sight was the burly water-backs which heave after heave kept tumbling up from the broken foam and their plump heap turning open in ropes of velvet (J 200)

Inscape, when it reveals itself, is always a significant moment for Hopkins. A maternal uncle, (George Giberne), was a pioneering photographer and Hopkins uses the word 'caught' very much as a camera might 'capture' an elusive subject in a particular light, movement or posture. For Hopkins it is the immediacy which is important: 'looking out of my window I caught it [a particular inscape] in the random clods and broken heaps of snow made by the cast of a broom' (J 230), he writes; or 'I catch... the looped or forked wisp made by every big pebble the backwater runs over' (J 223). One of his most famous poems, 'The Windhover', begins with just such a momentary apprehension when he 'catches' the inscape of the hawk's flight.

Remembering the division of labour which produced his own and William Wordsworth's joint-authored collection of poems, *Lyrical Ballads* in 1798, Samuel Taylor Coleridge wrote:

Mr Wordsworth [...] was to propose to himself as his object, to give the charm of novelty to things of every day [...] by awakening the mind's attention from the lethargy of custom, and directing it to the loveliness and the wonders of the world before us; an inexhaustible treasure, but for which in consequence of the film of familiarity and selfish solicitude we have eyes, yet see not, ears that hear not, and hearts that neither feel nor understand'.[1]

Like Wordsworth, Hopkins attempts through his process of inscape to re-educate our sensibilities, making them alert to what otherwise might have gone unnoticed. So, in one particular journal entry, for example, he is admiring the construction of a barn roof and writes, 'I thought how sadly beauty of inscape was unknown and buried away from simple people and yet how near at hand it was if they had eyes to see it and it could be called out everywhere again' (J 221). Hopkins's heightened and subtle awareness of the world in which he lived made him acutely conscious of the delicacy of its organisation. In one journal entry he anticipates the subject of his own 'Binsey Poplars' when recording the felling of an ash tree: 'I heard the sound and looking out

---

1 *Biographia Literaria*, Chapter 14.

and seeing it maimed there came at that moment a great pang and I wished to die and not see the inscapes of the world destroyed any more' (J 230).

2.3   Inscape of Poetry

Inscape is a term which Hopkins applied not only to the distinctive patterns of individual things, but also to describe poetic style. This is particularly important for the poetry he himself writes: 'what I call *inscape*', he tells Patmore, 'is species or individuality – distinctive beauty of style' (FL 373). Hopkins's poetry, its shape and sound patterns, was the product of an intelligence developed apart from the mainstream culture and within the strict formalities and rules of a religious life, and he was aware, sometimes painfully, of the bafflement, and occasional hostility, that his poems provoked even among his few contemporary readers. 'You give me a long jobation about eccentricities', he tells Bridges wryly. 'Alas I have heard so much about and suffered so much for and in fact been so completely ruined for life by my alleged singularities that they are a sore subject' (LB 126). In an essay written for his tutor, T. H. Green, 'The Position of Plato to the Greek World', in which he looks at the relative orientation to their own worlds of Shakespeare and Wordsworth, he decides that Wordsworth 'is felt rather to express the contradiction to the spirit of his times, than to represent their tendencies' (J 115). Like Wordsworth, who talked of creating the taste by which he was to be enjoyed, Hopkins, too, had to struggle against the opinions of more conventional poets like Patmore and Bridges to establish his distinctive voice and an acceptance of his poetry's technical originality. He particularly deplored what he called 'Parnassian' in a poet, 'that is the language and style of poetry mastered and at command but employed without any fresh inspiration' (LD 72). To take poetry to new levels of inspiration Hopkins developed a range of expressive techniques. In his *Preface* to the edition of 1918 Robert Bridges notes that Hopkins was alive to oddities in his own verse but could not understand accusations of obscurity.[1] Among the liberties he accused him of taking with grammar, Bridges identified in Hopkins as a chief cause of his obscurity 'his habitual omission of the relative pronoun'. This is a recurrent stylistic device which is to be found in examples such as:

> The men [that]/Woke thee ('The Wreck of the Deutschland', st.25)

> After-comers cannot guess the beauty [that has] been
> ('Binsey Poplars')

---

1   Robert Bridges, Editor's Preface to Notes in Charles Williams, ed. *The Poems of Gerard Manley Hopkins* (Oxford: Oxford.University Press, 1930), p. 97

> Here! Creep, /Wretch, under a comfort [that] serves in a whirlwind
> ('No worst')

His poetry, Hopkins insisted, must be read as sound; it makes its impact primarily through the stress patterns of speech, 'Stress is the life of it' (LB 52). It is indeed possible to read the poetry for its pleasing patterns of sound alone which often carry the sense of the lines through their sheer musicality. Among his theories about poetry Hopkins described it as, 'Speech framed for contemplation of the mind by the way of hearing or speech framed to be heard for its own sake and interest even over and above its interest of meaning' (J 289). 'Verse', he said, is 'inscape of spoken sound, not spoken words' (J 289), and he believed his own poetry's lexical obscurities could be resolved by being heard. They would 'explode' into meaning, to use his own term (B 98): 'take breath and read it with the ears, as I always wish to be read', he writes, 'and my verse becomes all right'.[1] A difficult sonnet such as 'Harry Ploughman', for example, Hopkins described as 'altogether for recital, not for perusal (as by nature verse should be)' (LB 263) and of 'Spelt from Sibyl's Leaves' he wrote: 'Of this long sonnet above all remember what applies to all my verse, that it is, as living art should be, made for performance and that its performance is not reading with the eye but loud, leisurely, poetical (not rhetorical) recitation' (LB 246).

To these ends, therefore, Hopkins avoided the niceties of polite poetical speech which might prevent the direct communication of his readers with the experiences he wanted to describe. Wordsworth, in his *Advertisement* to *Lyrical Ballads* (1798) is a precedent for poets who wished to escape a tutored diction and take poetry back to its origins in the real language of men and oral culture. Hopkins himself was particularly interested in and influenced by the literatures of, for example, Old Norse, Icelandic, Anglo-Saxon and Welsh traditions. For him the true test of poetic language was its effectiveness primarily as the spoken word, as speech-sound:

> I cut myself off from the use of *ere, o'er, wellnigh, what time, say not* (for *do not say*)', he wrote to Bridges, 'because, though dignified, they neither belong to nor ever cd. arise from, or be the elevation of, ordinary modern speech. For it seems to me that the poetical language of an age shd. be the current language heightened (LB 89)

In reading Hopkins's poetry it is impossible to miss the measures and cadences of the speaking voice, for example:

---

1   Robert Bridges, *ibid.*, p.97

Ah, touched in your bower of bone
Are you! Turned for an exquisite smart,
Have you! Make words break from me here all alone,
Do you!
Why, tears! Is it? Tears; such a melting, a madrigal start!
          ('The Wreck of the Deutschland' st.18)
Ah well, God rest him all road ever he offended
          ('Felix Randal')

O what black hours we have spent
This night! What sights you, heart, saw, ways you went!
          ('I wake and feel')

Chief among his many technical devices, all contributing to the sound patterns of his verse are:

Parallelisms (traceable to biblical patterns and Old English forms): 'With the gnarls of the nails in thee, niche of the lance' ('The Wreck of the Deutschland' st.23)

Lettering of syllables (J 283) which include alliteration, internal and half-rhyme: 'And frightful a nightfall folded rueful a day' ('The Wreck of the Deutschland'st.15)

Compound adjectives, either simple: 'dapple-dawn-drawn Falcon' ('The Windhover') or complex: 'tumbled over rim in roundy wells/Stones' ('As kingfishers catch fire')

Omission or displacement of prepositions: 'Some candle clear burns some-where [as] I come by' ('The Candle Indoors'). 'Your offering, with despatch, of' [make your offering of this, quickly] ('Morning, Midday, and Evening Sacrifice')

Inversions of word order: 'Hold them cheap/ May who ne'er hung there' [Those who never hung there may well hold them cheap] ('No worst')

Vowel chime (what Hopkins called 'vowelling off'): 'like each tucked string tells, each hung bell's/ Bow swung finds tongue to fling out broad its name' ('As kingfishers catch fire')

Repetition of alliterating consonants (from Hopkins's study of a Welsh form called *cynghanedd*, pronounced *kung-hanneth*): 'To bathe in his fall-gold mercies, to breathe in his all-fire glances' ('The Wreck of the Deutschland' st.23)

Inscape, therefore, is an essential part of Hopkins's style and poetics. 'Poetry is in fact speech', he wrote, 'only employed to carry the inscape of speech for inscape's sake – and therefore the inscape must be dwelt on' (J 283) There is a 'Modernist' resonance in Hopkins's definition of poetry as something 'framed to be heard for its own sake and interest over and above its interest of meaning' (J 289) prefiguring, for example, Archibald MacLeish's 'a poem should not mean/But be' ('Ars Poetica', 1926). Hopkins writes that, to poetry, 'Some matter and meaning is essential...but only as an element necessary to support and employ the shape which is contemplated for its own sake' (J 289). In statements of this kind he looks on to figures like E. E. Cummings and to twentieth century concrete poetry, as well as anticipating remarks such as those of William Carlos Williams, 'A poem is a small (or large) machine made of words' ('Prepositions', 19).

Hopkins favoured the sonnet and thirty-four of his sixty-five complete poems are in this form. He did, however, take the liberty of modifying the traditional fourteen lines by writing sometimes what he called a 'curtal' sonnet, as in 'Pied Beauty' with its six lines for the traditional octave, four lines for the sestet, and a half-line tailpiece. Another of his variations is 'Tom's Garland', a sonnet with two additions of two and a half lines each making up one coda, while 'Spelt from Sibyl's Leaves' he called 'the longest sonnet ever made' (LB 245). Hopkins's sonnets have such intensity and compression that the form itself is given new possibilities of expressiveness.

2.4 Instress

In an early notebook discussion of the Greek philosopher, Parmenides, Hopkins makes use of another term which he regards as coterminous with 'inscape'. The inscapes of all things, in the way Parmenides' meaning is here applied, are upheld by instress 'and are meaningless without it', he writes. Without instress there would be 'no bridge, no stem of stress between us and things to bear us out and carry the mind over' (J 127). Instress is for Hopkins here a form of energy which keeps a thing what that thing is and not some other possible thing, a 'stress' which is inseparable from the inscape of something and which must be apprehended with it for that thing to be truly *inscaped*. Instress is therefore within the mind of the poet as well as in the object of his attention. In a journal entry of 1872, Hopkins writes typically of what a distraction a companion is for him in his attempt to 'catch' the 'thisness' ('haeccitas') of the grass he is looking at:

> Green-white tufts of long bleached grass like heads of hair or the crowns of heads of hair, each a whorl of slender curves, one tuft taking up another - however these I might have noticed any day. I saw the inscape though freshly, as if my eye were still growing, though with a companion the eye and the ear are for the most part shut and instress cannot come' (J 228).

Instress is therefore an indispensable part of the inscaping process. The experience of inscape always depends more than on simply what the eye looks at. So, for example, in observing the breakers on a shoreline Hopkins writes: 'About all the turns of the scaping from the break and flooding of wave to its run out again I have not yet satisfied myself' (J 223). Clearly there is a visual adequacy, but the lagging satisfaction implies that he feels something missing in his responsiveness. There is a similarity here to the way in which Coleridge refers to his experience of natural objects in 'Dejection: an Ode': 'I see them all, so excellently fair! / I see, not feel, how beautiful they are (ll.42-3). And Wordsworth in *The Prelude* is close to Hopkins's instress when he speaks of the reciprocity between poet and object as:

> A balance, an ennobling interchange
> Of action from within and from without,
> The excellence, pure spirit, and best power
> Both of the object seen, and eye that sees.[1]

For Hopkins instress is the significant principle which upholds the very being of inscape. In a letter to Patmore in 1883, in which he is discussing tone, pitch and stress, he reveals how close in his mind is the relationship between stress and inscape. Stress, he writes, 'is the making a thing more, or making it markedly, what it already is; it is the bringing out its nature' (FL 327). So, in 'Hurrahing in Harvest', for example, Hopkins inscapes the autumnal landscape, first bringing out visually the 'lovely behaviour/Of silk-sack clouds' and asking 'has wilder, wilful-wavier/Meal-drift moulded ever and melted across skies?' It is only when he can apprehend with his own mind the instress, here coming to be recognised as the pervasive energy of Creation's God ('And the azurous hung hills are his world-wielding shoulder/Majestic – as a stallion stalwart'), that Hopkins can sense a Wordsworthian reciprocity between 'action from within and from without', taking him to a moment of supreme joy:

---

1   *The Prelude*, 1805, xii, ll.576–9

These things, these things were here and but the beholder
Wanting; which two when they once meet,
The heart rears wings bold and bolder
And hurls for him, O half hurls earth for him off under his feet.

In the natural world or in a work of art, therefore, instress is the organisational energy or principle which binds together, on the one hand, the particularities of inscapes and, on the other, the mind in its cognitive apprehension of them. In 'Pied Beauty' Hopkins describes diversity brought to a unity in the mind of God. In his poetry he looks for that instress which makes sense both of creation and of his own experience of it. God's 'mystery' must not only be 'instressed', as he says in 'The Wreck of the Deutschland', but it must also be 'stressed' (1.39), that is articulated or 'worded' (1.230). Without the cohesive sense of instress the universe becomes, as Coleridge describes it, only 'an immense heap of *little* things'.[1] With what he called the 'coad-unating' imagination Coleridge, too, strove to reconcile 'opposite or discordant qualities'[2] and bring all into a state of oneness: 'My mind feels as if it ached to behold & know something *great* – something *one & indivisible*'. To lose this sense of wholeness was to suffer Coleridgean 'dejection' as happened to Hopkins at Stonyhurst in August, 1873: 'I was quite downcast: nature in all her parcels and faculties gaped and fell apart, *fatiscebat*, like a clod cleaving and holding by strings of root' (J 236). For Hopkins, instress was that necessary awareness at all times of God's unifying, indwelling presence in creation.

2.5 Sprung Rhythm

Writing to Dixon in 1878 Hopkins described how, in 'The Wreck of the Deutschland' three years previously, he had been able to realise a new rhythm which had been 'haunting' his ear for a long time (LD 14). Prosodic issues are at the heart of his poetry which is primarily concerned with stress and sound pattern, and his deployment of diacritical marks indicating where he felt the stresses should fall in the lines of his poem was one of several 'oddnesses' (ibid.) which he believed had led to its rejection by the Jesuit magazine, *The Month*.

   The term 'sprung rhythm', like 'inscape' and 'instress', has come to be exclusively associated with Hopkins, although as he himself pointed out in the same letter,

---

1   E. L. Griggs ed. *Collected Letters of Samuel Taylor Coleridge* (Oxford: Clarendon Press, 1956), Vol.1, p.349
2   *Biographia Literaria*, Chapter 14

there were many precedents for it, not only in major writers such as Shakespeare and Milton, but also in 'nursery rhymes and popular jingles' (ibid.). At the beginning of his *Author's Preface*[1] Hopkins announces that the poems in his book are written in a mixture of 'Running Rhythm' and 'Sprung Rhythm' and he clearly sets out what he means, first of all, by Running Rhythm – 'the common rhythm in English use'. Running Rhythm is measured by feet of either two or three syllables. Each foot has a principal 'Stress' (–) and the other one, or two, unstressed syllables make up what is called the 'Slack' (×). If the stress comes last in the metrical feet, these are called 'Falling Feet'. Where the stress comes first, they are 'Rising Feet'.

The four most common measures in English poetry are the iambic foot (×–) and the anapaestic foot (××–), both beginning with Slack syllables; and the trochaic (–×) and dactylic (–××) which begin with Stress syllables.

In sprung rhythm, as Hopkins explained to Dixon, scanning is by 'accents or stresses alone, without any account of the number of syllables, so that a foot may be one strong syllable or it may be many light and one strong' (LD 14). As ever, Hopkins has in mind the aural nature of his poetry. 'My verse is less to be read than heard,' he tells Bridges, and in the same letter explains that he uses sprung rhythm 'because it is the nearest to the rhythm of prose, that is the native and natural rhythm of speech' (LB 46). In a similar way Wordsworth had argued that there was no essential distinction between the language of prose and the language of metrical composition.[2] Hopkins makes 'stress' his guiding principle. Taking a line from his poem 'The Loss of the Eurydice' he points out that, '"she had come from a cruise training seamen" read without stress and declaim is mere Lloyd's Shipping Intelligence; properly read it is quite a different thing. Stress is the life of it' (LB 52). Aiming therefore for 'naturalness of expression' he asks, 'why, if it is forcible in prose to say "lashed rod", am I obliged to weaken this in verse, which ought to be stronger, not weaker, into "láshed birch-ród" or something?' (LB 46).

Sprung rhythm, therefore, as Hopkins explains in his *Author's Preface*, is 'measured by feet of from one to four syllables, regularly, and for particular effects any number of weak or slack syllables may be used'. A line in iambic pentameter in common running rhythm, therefore, might be:

×   – × – x – ×   – ×   –
The breezy call of incense-breathing Morn

---

1   Phillips, pp.106-9
2   Preface to *Lyrical Ballads*, 1800

A line in sprung rhythm, keeping five stresses but with 'any number' of unstressed syllables would read:

> ‒ × × × ‒ × × × × × ‒ × × ‒ × × × ‒ × ×
> Finger of a tender of, O of a feathery delicacy, the breast of the
>> ('The Wreck of the Deutschland'. St.31, l.16)

or an Alexandrine (six iambic feet) with 'any number' of unstressed syllables:

> ×× ‒ × × ‒ × × × × × ‒ × × ‒ × ×
> I awoke in the midsummer not-to-call night, in the white and the
>
> ‒ × × ‒ ×
> walk of the morning　　('Moonrise June 19, 1876')

Hopkins tells Dixon: 'I shd. add that the word Sprung which I use for this rhythm means something like *abrupt* and applies by rights only where one stress follows another running, without syllable between' (LD 23). His own instance of sprung rhythm in nursery rhyme adequately illustrates his point here:

> ‒ ‒ ‒ ‒ ‒ ‒ ‒ ‒ ‒ ‒ ‒
> "Ding, dong, bell; Pussy's in the well; Who put her in? Little Johnny Thin.
>
> ‒ ‒ ‒ ‒ ‒ ‒
> Who pulled her out? Little Johnny Stout" For if each line has three stresses or three feet it follows that some of the feet are of one syllable only (LD 14).

A line such as

> × ‒ ‒ ‒ × × ‒ ‒ ‒
> 'The sour scythe cringe, and the blear share come'[1]

has two sets of three stresses, one stress following another and running, as Hopkins told Dixon, 'without syllable between' (LD 23); the effect being, appropriately in the context of this particular stanza, that of a sudden and abrupt springing of a trap on the unsuspecting reader who is blithely heedless of 'Death' awaiting him.

　　After writing 'The Wreck of the Deutschland', Hopkins told Dixon, he felt himself free to compose and tried 'various other experiments – as "outriding feet" that is parts of which do not count in the scanning' (LD 15). They are so called, he wrote, 'because they seem to hang below the line or ride forward or backward from it in another dimension than the line itself' (*Author's Preface*). An example of outriding feet would be:

1　'The Wreck of the *Deutschland',* st.11, l.18

    ×   —   ×   —   —   × —
The heart rears wings bold and bolder

  ×   —   ×   —   —   —   — × × ×   —
And hurls <u>for him</u> O half hurls earth <u>for him</u> off under his feet

                                 ('Hurrahing in Harvest')

Some of his sonnets, he goes on to tell Dixon, he has written 'in the ordinary scanning counterpointed' (LD 15), that is where a line has 'two different coexisting scansions' (ibid.). The example Hopkins gives of counterpointing is from Milton where to read:

      —   —   —   —   —
'"*Home to* his mother's house *private* returned"' (ibid.)

makes more sense in terms of the speaking voice than to scan it as regular iambic pentameter:

    ×   — × — ×   —   × — × —
'Home to his mother's house private returned'.[1]

Similarly, in two examples from Hopkins, it is

    —   —   —   ×   ×   —   ×   — × ×
By that window what task what fingers ply,

not

    ×   —   ×   —   ×   —   ×   — ×   —
By that window what task what fingers ply,

and

   — × ×   —   ×   — × × —   ×   —
Innocent mind and Mayday in girl and boy,

rather than

    × — ×   —   ×   — × × — ×   —
Innocent mind and Mayday in girl and boy,

Finally, among the many other prosodic strategies Hopkins employs is his technique of 'overeaving'. It is natural, he says, 'in Sprung Rhythm for the lines to be *rove over*, that is for the scanning of each line immediately to take up that of the one before' (*Author's Preface*). This is clear in a poem such as 'The Windhover' where the scansion continues over from one line to the next:

---

1   *Paradise Regained*, IV, l.639

× — × — × — × — × —
I caught this morning morning's minion king-

× × — × — × × × — × — × × — ×
dom of daylight's dauphin, dapple-dawn-drawn Falcon, in his riding

× × — × × × × × — × — × — × — ×
Of the rolling level underneath him steady air, and striding

— × × × — × × × — × × — × —
High there, how he rung upon the rein of a wimpling wing

× × — × ×
In his ecstasy!

Were these lines to be separated from each other as discrete units of meaning, the effect would be lost of 'the roll, the rise, the carol'[1] of the windhover in its flight, to which the 'rove over' scansion and sprung rhythm so marvellously contribute.

---

1   'To R. B.'

Part 3. Reading Hopkins

The material in this section should be read in conjunction with the text. It is not intended to be read as a free-standing 'account' of the poems.

3.1 'The Wreck of the Deutschland'[1]

Hopkins sent 'The Wreck of the Deutschland' (together with 'The Loss of the Eurydice') to Canon Dixon for his comments on 29 March 1879. He wrote: 'please return them when done with, as I have no other copies' (LD 26). It is terrifying to think that these works, one of them a masterpiece of nineteenth century poetry, could have been lost in the post! *The Wreck* was prompted by the Rector of St Bueno's remark that he wished someone would write a poem on the subject of the drowning (in the North Sea at the mouth of the Thames in 1875) of five Franciscan nuns exiled from Germany under Chancellor Bismarck's anti-Catholic laws (the Falck Laws) (LD 14). Up until this point and what he took to be a clear signal from his order that to write poetry would be a legitimate pursuit, Hopkins had kept to his self-imposed vow of poetic silence (LD 14).

When *The Wreck* was first submitted to the Jesuit journal, *The Month*, its editor, Henry Coleridge, promised to publish it. However, when Hopkins insisted on the retention of diacritical marks, placed to ensure that readers stressed the lines as he had intended, the poem was refused and remained unpublished until Bridges's edition in 1918. Bridges described the poem as 'a great dragon folded in the gate to forbid all entrance', and Father Clement Barraud in his 'Reminiscences of Father Gerard Hopkins', wrote:

> It has been said – he used to say it himself – that his verses need for proper appreciation to be read aloud by one who has mastered their eccentricities. Well, I heard the bard himself read parts of "The Wreck of the Deutschland", which he was writing at the time, and could understand hardly one line of it.[2]

---

1   A superb reading of this poem by Paul Scofield on audio cassette can be bought from http://www.mediasleuth.com

2   [Fr] C[lement] B[arraud], 'Reminiscences of Father Gerard Hopkins', *Month*, August 1919, cited from

Perhaps it is now less puzzling to readers, after almost a century for its ellipses of thought and its innovations of metre and vocabulary to have become the familiar discourse of poetry, but it is clear that the poem presented formidable difficulties at first. Arthur Clutton-Brock in *The Times Literary Supplement* of 9 January 1919 wrote: 'For Hopkins poetry meant difficulty; he wrote it to say more than could be said otherwise; it was for him a packing of words with sense, both emotional and intellectual'.[1] Hopkins told Bridges: 'One of two kinds of clearness one shd. have – either the meaning to be felt without effort as fast as one reads or else, if dark at first reading, when once made out *to explode*' (LB 90). Of *The Wreck*, he wrote: 'Granted that it needs study and is obscure, for indeed I was not over-desirous that the meaning of all should be quite clear' (LB 50). Such a statement, it might be said, is that of an original and often misunderstood poetic genius, and is anticipated in a famous remark of William Blake in a letter of 1799: 'You say that I want someone to Elucidate my Ideas. But you ought to know that What is Grand is necessarily obscure to Weak men. That which can be made Explicit to the Idiot is not worth my care'.[2]

Part the first

Stanza 1

God is acknowledged as the sustainer of life's necessities ('breath and bread'), as a safe shore ('strand'), yet also, in this 'shipwreck' poem, as the dynamic power behind the sea's movement, as well as its ruler ('sway'). In terms which recall John Donne's line, 'Thou hast made me, And shall thy work decay'? Hopkins is puzzled that his Creator had seemed almost determined to destroy him in a recent personal and spiritual crisis from which he has now emerged.[3] He casts himself here in the role of a very young child who feels for and finds the finger of its parent. Throughout the poem Hopkins will emphasise God's fatherly care which is often concealed behind the rigours of his dealings with his people.

Gerald Roberts ed. *Gerard Manley Hopkins: The Critical Heritage* (London: Thames & Hudson, 1981) p.130

1   Arthur Clutton-Brock, unsigned review, *Times Literary Supplement*, 9 January 1919, p.19, cited from Gerald Roberts, p.84

2   Letter to the Reverend John Trusler, August 23, 1799. M. L. Johnson & J. E. Grant eds. *Blake's Poetry and Designs* (London & New York: Norton, 1979), p.448

3   John Donne, 'Holy Sonnet 1'

Stanza 2

Now changing his role, perhaps to that of schoolboy, Hopkins has experienced those rigours, the 'lashed rod' which caused him to 'confess' – a situation similar to that of a confrontation with his headmaster ('Thou mastering me l.1) at Highgate School who 'blazed into me with his riding whip' (FL 2). He anticipates a submission later described in 'Carrion Comfort' when 'I kissed the rod, / Hand rather'. This stanza prefigures the sonnets of desolation in several ways – the individual dark night of the soul (1.5), the physical strain and 'stress' (1.8), as well as the almost tangible experience of being hurled and trodden (1.6) by a forceful deity (cf. 'The hero whose heaven-handling flung me, foot trod/ Me' ['Carrion Comfort']).

Stanza 3

In a nightmarish predicament, the 'hurtle of hell' (cf. 'cliffs of fall' in 'No worst') lies 'Behind', in front is God's 'frown'. The panic, in line three, of not knowing where to turn is relieved by a sudden surprising ability to escape on wings 'that spell' (that 'period of time'). The flight is achieved with the resolution of difficulty we associate with old-fashioned adventure stories, or perhaps cartoon films: 'I whirled out wings' ('with one bound Jack was free!'). Remarkably, the poet's heart (cf. 'hard at bay' st.7, with a semi-pun on 'hart') flies *at* ('fling') rather than away *from* its apparent adversary with the instinct of a homing pigeon ('Carrier-witted') ascending high above the dangers of the ground ('tower') to find its true domicile in Christ's Real Presence, 'the Host'.

Stanza 4

The poet is here sand in an hourglass, apparently firm ('fast') at the 'wall' but in reality a 'drift' and heading for 'the fall'. Possibly Christ's words are recalled here of the 'foolish man, which built his house upon the sand [...] and it fell: and great was the fall of it'. The wise man's house 'fell not: for it was founded upon a rock' (Matthew, Ch. 7,v. 24–7). Later, in stanza twenty-nine, the heroic nun of the wreck is that rock or 'Simon Peter of a soul', referring to Peter or the 'rock' upon which Christ built his own 'house', the Catholic or universal Church (Matthew, Ch.16, v.18). Fortunately, Hopkins's 'drift' steadies ('I steady') and he now becomes a well of water with a pane-like surface replenished constantly by the grace of what Christ's gospel offers ('proffer'), as though by streams trickling down a hillside ('voel'). These streams of truth are like ropes ('roped with') keeping him, as though he were a climber, *truly* fastened – unlike ropes of sand only *apparently* 'at the wall/ Fast'.

Stanza 5

With a flourishing gesture of assent (cf. 'I did say yes', st.2) and admiration Hopkins salutes God in his 'lovely asunder/Starlight' (cf. 'God's Grandeur') and in the 'dappled-with-damson west' (cf. Wordsworth's , 'Whose dwelling is the light of setting suns' ['Tintern Abbey'])[1], acknowledging that his energy, his 'instress' or presence that keeps inscapes in being, must be 'stressed' or proclaimed. Perhaps it is even best felt when 'stressed', that is, under stress, as both the poet in his recent experience and the five nuns in Part II equally know. The poet is always ready to respond to God's mysterious presence and to bless it in gratitude whenever he feels that he understands something of its mystery.

Stanza 6

This stanza consolidates an idea in the previous one that the source of God's felt presence ('stress') is not 'bliss'. Or that it is to be traced necessarily (a popular misconception being that 'heaven' causes them) to natural misfortunes – those things that can, and do, assuage guilt and 'melt' hard hearts. The 'stress felt' overrides all time as a vessel rides a river and 'here' (in other words what the next stanza is about to say) while the 'faithless' have no conception of it, or get it wrong, even the 'faithful' find it testing of their faith.

Stanza 7

The 'stress felt' derives from the time of Christ's life in Palestine, from his birth, infancy, passion and death, to his burial (through his resurrection) of that colourless natural existence from which mankind was yet *to* be born ('Warm-laid grave of a womb-life grey'- note the triple alliteration forcing the ideas together). In imagery reminiscent of 'God's Grandeur' the 'discharge' and 'swelling to be' of Christ's mission imply both electrical discharge – 'The world is charged with the grandeur of God' – and the gathering 'to a greatness [of] the ooze of oil'. The often remarked-upon notional discharge of electricity between the outstretched forefingers of Adam and God, his creator, in Michelangelo's Sistine Chapel painting has possible relevance to this poem with the finger of God prominent in stanzas one and thirty-one.[2]

---

1   *Lyrical Ballads*, 1798
2   The painting can be seen on the Web at http://www.teslasociety.com/art.htm

Though God's 'stress' was felt before the time of his incarnation, and though it continues powerfully to be so in the activities of his Christian followers, only those who suffer as he did can truly express it. And that 'expression' of Hopkins, a hard-won and strenuous assertion, is reserved for the opening words of the next stanza – 'Is out with it!'

Stanza 8

Depending on how it is perceived this 'last' of Hopkins can be regarded as his 'best or worst/ Word'. Either way, it is felt as a 'lash', but the 'lashed rod' of stanza two turned out to be a benison, just as later, in stanza twenty-four, the suffering nun 'christens her wild-worst Best'. There follows an image which probably derives from Keats's 'Ode on Melancholy' where the peculiar pleasure to be found in pain can be experienced only by 'him whose strenuous tongue/ Can burst Joy's grape against his palate fine'. Hopkins takes the bittersweet sloe as a 'type' of the body of Christ whose 'flesh-burst'/destruction instantly floods the mouth/man with sweetness. Men, whether they are 'sour or sweet', are drawn to the feet of the crucified Christ regardless of intention, will or warning. This stanza is typical of how Hopkins tests the limits of language's potential to ensure that particular 'intensity' which Keats regarded as 'the excellence of every art'.[1] Here, for example, he makes use of tmesis, splitting a compound, as in 'Brim, in a flash, full!' and separating a noun from its apostrophe by incorporating another noun within the possessive 's': 'To hero of Calvary, Christ,'s feet'.

Stanza 9

This stanza is both imperative and an imprecation demanding that God, in the form of the Trinity, ensures his own adoration and inviting him to treat stubborn ('dogged') man with various modes of salutary forcefulness. In terms which consolidate the 'argument' up to this point God's true nature is displayed in paradoxical couplings – 'lightning and love', 'a winter and warm', 'Father and fondler' – as most merciful when appearing most terrible. Soon these truths will be demonstrated through Hopkins's interpretation of the sufferings of the five nuns on the *Deutschland*, but the previous stanzas are based upon his own experience ('I found it') of a sweetness beyond even the capacity of someone with his linguistic resourcefulness to describe, 'Beyond saying [...] past telling of tongue'.

---

1   'The excellence of every art is its intensity', Letter, 21 December 1917

Stanza 10

Hopkins asks God to master 'Man's malice' either by beating him into shape as though on an anvil (cf. Donne: 'bend/ Your force, to breake, blow, burn and make me new'),[1] or by more gentle means, as Spring slowly dissolves the ice of winter – 'melt him but master him still'. Wordsworth in *The Prelude* describes two similar procedures in the growth and formation of his own mind, Nature either 'seeking him/With gentlest visitation' or sometimes needing to employ 'Severer interventions'.[2] Hopkins's historical precedents here are the sudden and violent conversion of St Paul on the road to Damascus (Acts, Ch. ix, v.1–6) and the more gradual and gentle progress of St Augustine towards faith.

The poem, at the end of stanza ten, recalls its beginning. Hopkins's acknowledgment of God's mastery over him is developed into a prayer that he will now make 'out of us all/ Mastery'. This self-contained unit of personal experience gives way here to a narrative. Wordsworth had said that in the poems of his collection, *Lyrical Ballads*, 'the feeling therein developed [gave] importance to the action and situation, and not the action and situation to the feeling'.[3] One might compare the remarks of Hopkins in a letter to Bridges: 'The Deutschland would be more generally interesting if there were more wreck and less discourse, I know, but still it is an ode and not primarily a narrative'. And referring to Pindar in this connection he acknowledged 'some narrative [...] but the principle (sic) business is lyrical' (LB 49).

Part the second

Stanza 11

As if in procession, 'Death' beats a drum and proclaims various ways in which men might meet with him. It could be traditionally through war, fire, attack by wild animals, or drowning, or it could be the more contemporary fate of being struck by a railway train ('flange and the rail'). With the high wind of 'Storms', as in the one about to be described, 'Death' blows a triumphant 'bugle' as though announcing his victory. Yet despite all the evidence ('Flesh falls within sight of us'), we blithely 'dream' that our stay on earth is permanent and 'forget' that we must be reaped by the 'sour scythe' as we 'cringe' humbly before it and are ploughed under by the 'share' whose poor-

1   John Donne, 'Holy Sonnet XIV'
2   *The Prelude*, 1805, 1, ll.566–7, 570
3   Preface to *Lyrical Ballads*, 1800

sightedness ('blear') makes it indiscriminate in its actions.

J. M. W.Turner. 'SnowStorm - Steamboat off a Harbour's Mouth' (1842)'
Wiry and white-fiery and whirlwind-swivelled snow
© Tate Gallery, London, 2005

Stanza 12

The narrative begins. The *Deutschland* puts out from 'Bremen' (Bremerhaven) with a complement of about ('tell in the round') two hundred people heading for what, with hindsight, might have seemed a predestined fate – 'The goal [...] the doom to be drowned'. Still ('yet') their exposure ('not under thy feathers') to the elements was only apparently God's 'dark side' but in reality his 'bay' or shelter, the stormy sky a 'vault' or cover, and his mercy something to fasten ('reeve') 'even them in'.

Stanza 13

In leaving Bremerhaven ('Hurling the Haven behind') the nun-heroine of the poem will eventually reach, through death, 'the heaven-haven of the reward' (st.35). 'Heaven-Haven', subtitled 'a nun takes the veil', is the title of an early poem by Hopkins (1864) where the postulant asks 'to be/ Where no storms come' and 'out of the swing of the sea' (cf. 'sway of the sea' l.3).[1] The 'reward' which awaits the nun of the *Deutschland*, however, can only be achieved through the grim endurance of tribulation. A famous remark of Milton's is relevant here: 'I cannot praise a fugitive and cloistered virtue, unexercised and unbreathed, that never sallies out and sees her adversary, but slinks out of the race, where that immortal garland is to be run for, not without dust and heat'.[2] With characteristic virtuosity Hopkins uses alliterative techniques, vowel chime and internal rhymes to re-create the confusion of the elements as the air, cooperating with the 'widow-making unchilding unfathering deeps' undoes the bonds of kinship ('unkind'). Here he echoes the Anglo-Saxon kenning for the sea: 'widowmaker'.

Stanza 14

The *Deutschland* is grounded on the Kentish Knock, a submerged sandbank at the mouth of the Thames. Misled by night she is drawn 'Dead' (straight, or fatally) onto its ridges ('combs'). The six stresses in the final line effectively demonstrate the vulnerability of sails, disengaged propeller ('whorl') and ship's wheel to the 'ruinous shock' of the waves.

Stanza 15

In the briefest of reflective pauses the stanza presents personified 'Hope' as a 'carved' stone monumental figure (like Shakespeare's 'Patience on a monument')[3] upon whose cheeks the watery tracks of tears have 'Trenched' channels. The thrice repeated 'Hope' is juxtaposed with details whose effect in the process of reading is to cancel the very meaning of it, 'grey hairs', 'mourning', 'tears', 'cares', 'despair'. At this point it is possible that Hopkins may have had in mind Longfellow's celebrated poem, 'The Wreck of the Hesperus' (1840). In his other poem about a shipwreck, 'The Loss of the Eurydice', the virtue 'Faith', like Hope, is similarly compromised,

---

1 Phillips, p.27
2 *Areopagitica*
3 *Twelfth Night*, 2, iv, 114

'And you were a liar, O blue March day' (l.21). However, Charity, the greatest of St Paul's three virtues, emerges finally to be celebrated at the triumphant conclusion of *The Wreck* where Christ becomes its embodiment (st.35, and see Paul, Cor. Ch.13). The narrative resumes with a masterful line (l.5) whose vowel chime creates a dirge-like resonance, while words such as 'shrouds' for rigging, and passengers 'folded' by night like sheep for the slaughter, add to the general sense of foreboding. Even here, however, 'folding' implies the ongoing care of a Good Shepherd always observant of and tending to his endangered flock.

Stanza 16

Many of the details in the poem, as in this particular stanza's description of the sailor's bravery, were drawn from Hopkins's reading of accounts of the wreck in *The Times* and *Illustrated London News*.[1] The sailor, overwhelmed by the storm, has 'braids of thew', reminiscent of the subject of 'Harry Ploughman', while the 'dandled' corpse and 'cobbled foam-fleece' are words we associate, perhaps, with the happy movements of an infant and with softness, but which are incongruously employed here in a situation of horror and hardship. There is a callous, almost playful, vitality in nature's destructive heedlessness implicit in 'fountains', 'buck', and in the next stanza's 'sea-romp'.

Stanza 17

The parentheses of line three create simultaneous multiple actions which contribute to the overall sense of mayhem. Even in such extremity, however, we are not allowed to forget the guiding divine presence in 'God's cold'. Night 'roared' as though itself heartbroken to hear the 'wailing' and 'crying' of, by this time, a confused 'rabble' of sufferers. Emergent is the figure of the 'tall nun' (st.19), a 'prophetess towered in the tumult'. Her tongue, like a bell in a bell-tower, 'told' a prophecy while it also, perhaps, 'tolled' for the dead. As tower, she replaces the Old Testament 'Tower of Babel' ('babble' l.17) with the *clear* word of God that she will soon utter unequivocally ('outright', st.30). As helpless, virginal female she is endowed, paradoxically, with the strength of a 'lioness'.

Stanza 18

Absent from the poem since stanza ten Hopkins here reintroduces himself. The nar-

---

1   *The Times*, 11 December 1875; *Illustrated London News*, 18 December 1875

rative has affected him deeply and, addressing his heart in its 'bower of bone' (cf. 'bone-house', 'The Caged Skylark'), he recognises that his tears are 'uttering truth' about the true nature of the heart. In King Lear, Cordelia, too, ('Cor' – Latin, 'heart'), expresses her truthful self not in language but through her heartfelt emotions, her smiles and tears (4, iii, 17–22). Her 'unteachably after evil' sisters are more verbally adept. There is a Keatsian 'exquisite smart' in Hopkins's pleasure as he melts to this expressively beautiful impulse ('madrigal start'). The sense by this stage is of tragedy being converted into an occasion for 'revel', 'glee' and 'good'.

Stanza 19

The nun calls on her 'master' with the additional sense of Christ as the real ship's master. Blinded physically by the smarting brine she 'sees one thing', as Gloucester in *King Lear* who, though blinded physically, comes to a better spiritual 'sight'. Her voice overrides the noise of the elements which are slogging and 'brawling' like an unruly mob (informed perhaps by Hopkins's own fear of the mob; see 'Tom's Garland' commentary).

Stanza 20

The nun was foremost of five wearing the head-dress (coifèd) of their order. Hopkins remarks that 'Deutschland' is 'double a desperate name!' being not only the name of the ill-fated vessel but also the country whose 'Falck Laws' have driven the nuns into exile. Falck was Bismarck's Minister of Culture under whose anti-Catholic policies the Church had been seriously weakened in Germany. However, Hopkins acknowledges that both good and evil, as often happens in life, can come from the same source. Cain and Abel shared a mother, Eve, while St Gertrude ('Christ's lily') and the Protestant Luther (to the Catholic Hopkins the 'beast of the waste wood') inhabited the same town of Eisleben.

Stanza 21

Protestant England seems equally inhospitable as the *Deutschland* has foundered at the mouth of London's River Thames. These nuns were on their way to settle in America, and England's moral responsibility for their misfortune is perhaps shared with that of Germany and might justifiably be laid also 'at our door' (st.35). Hopkins brings in an astronomical figure, Orion, the Hunter, whose hunting dogs, Canis Major (leading star, Sirius, 'the dog star') and Canis Minor (leading star, Procyon) accompany him on his journey round the sky. Like dogs, 'Surf, snow, river and earth/ Gnashed' at these suffering souls, but Hopkins sees God as an 'Orion of light', that is, the *true* hunter of men, who is 'weighing the worth' of each. At his 'unchancelling' hands (with a glancing pun on 'chancellor') the nuns are liberated from their chancel, screening them even in church and maintaining their privacy by separating them off from the rest of the congregation. Now enfranchised, their names are written visibly on the 'scroll-leaved flowers' of snow flakes, giving them equal status with those figures of myth who were taken from earth to become constellations forever on public view.

Stanza 22

Hopkins, whose mathematical abilities lie behind his contribution to Manley Hopkins's book *The Cardinal Numbers* (1887), here concerns himself with the multiple significance of the number 'five'. Part One of the poem has twice five stanzas; part two, five by five. 'Five' was the number or outward mark ('sake' cf. 'Henry Purcell' l.10) and 'cipher' (symbol) of Christ through his five wounds. We are asked to 'mark' (notice) that this 'mark' is our doing (cf. Blake's usage, wandering the city streets to 'mark' (notice) ... the bloody 'Marks of ... woe' ('London'). The wounds of the suffering Christ have sometimes been bestowed as visible marks or stigmata on his 'bespoken', those specially chosen from all eternity ('Before-time-taken'), just as they were on St Francis, founder of the Franciscan order to which these five nuns belong. In the final line Hopkins connects the red rose, as symbol of martyrdom, with the reddle (red dye) marking the fleece of the sacrificial lamb, symbol of Christ, the martyred Lamb of God.

Stanza 23

The stigmata, or visible 'Lovescape' of the crucified Christ, was the 'seal' on St Francis or guarantee on earth of his later arrival as 'seraph' into heaven. So the five nuns are 'sealed' for Christ by a total baptismal immersion in the 'wild waters' of the stormy sea. But the waves as a terrible manifestation of God's power conceal in reality his 'fall-gold mercies'.

Stanza 24

Hopkins now withdraws from the immediacy of the storm to reflect on his own then comparatively tranquil situation at St Bueno's College in North Wales. He focuses especially on the cry of the nun as reported in *The Times* of Saturday, 11 December 1875 – 'O Christ, come quickly'. By recognising God's presence in the storm the nun saw her 'Best' hope in this 'worst' of situations.

Stanza 25

This stanza, together with the next two, tries to interpret the nun's call – 'what did she mean?' Hopkins invokes the Holy Spirit, the 'original breath', to inspire him (cf. Milton, *Paradise Lost*, 1, 17–22). Was it, perhaps, that she wanted, like Christ, to die and rise again? (He now calls on Christ himself for aid – 'Breathe body of lovely Death'). If this were so then the apostles who woke the sleeping Christ as they feared to drown in the 'weather of Gennésaréth' were 'else-minded' (Matt., 8, 25). Was it perhaps that the nun was 'keener' to reach comfort through death because of the inimical cold ('keen') she was feeling? It is also worth considering the term 'keen' in the light of some modern criticism which interprets the Christ-nun relationship as sexual.[1]

Stanza 26

The nun's blessed relief is compared to the emergence of beautiful May-time blue skies from downy-breasted ('down-dugged') ground fog, and to the gentle glow at night of the 'moth-soft Milky Way'. This natural beauty, to be found similarly described in 'Spring' and 'The Starlight Night' is evidence of God's greater glory within and behind it. Hopkins adapts St Paul (Cor.1, Ch.2, v.9.) who, in terms which recall his own 'past telling of tongue' (st.9), challenges our 'eyesight' and 'hearing' to supply even the remotest conception of the 'treasure' which awaits us in heaven.

Stanza 27

None of these speculations provides an answer to the question posed in stanza twenty-five. It is not 'danger' which causes the nun to ask for 'ease'. Rather is it the bumpy progress on the rough road of life, the weariness which 'Time' imposes on the sorrow-saturated heart. And although a nun's life of quiet meditation on the 'Passion' of Christ would be more appealing to the heart ('it'), Hopkins imagines ('I gather') that this particular nun's mind, in her suffering extremity, was otherwise preoccupied, and not by choice.

Stanza 28

The sequence of ellipses which opens this stanza (cf. st.3) creates an urgent, breath-less attempt, as though Hopkins struggles through an obstructing crowd ('make me room there'), to get to the very meaning at the centre of all existence, Christ himself

---

1   See Part 4, 'Reception', & *Hamlet*, 3, ii , 249

('Ipse'). Christ, the nun's 'pride', is encouraged to exercise his mastery and bring her ordeal to an end. He is imaged as a triumphal horseman (now replacing the processional triumph of 'Death' in stanza eleven) just as later, in stanza thirty-five, he will become 'chivalry's [...] Lord', as he becomes Hopkins's own 'chevalier' in 'The Windhover'.

Stanza 29

The nun's interpretation, her 'wording', of the apparently senseless or 'unshapeable' events of that particular night, is accurate as she understands both 'Heaven and earth' to be the 'word' of God, and all nature, in fact, as given expression by ('worded by') him. She is immoveable before the 'blast' or winds of destruction like Christ's 'rock' and founder of his Church, St Peter, or the 'Tarpeian' rock of Rome's Capitol; Rome being now, of course, no longer pagan but the seat of Papal power and authority. Continuing with his metaphor of the tall nun as a tower (st.17), Hopkins here makes her into a sea-mark or lighthouse, like Shakespeare's 'ever-fixed mark/That looks on tempests and is never shaken' (Sonnet 116). Or she is a wind-fanned fire beacon whose light is the saviour of souls in distress, to be contrasted with the 'rocket and lightship' which were ineffective in bringing 'rescue' in stanza fifteen.

Stanza 30

Hopkins asks Jesus, 'heart's light', to give him some sense of the feast in heaven following the nun's arrival there. The wreck of the *Deutschland*, on the night of the sixth and seventh of December 1875 coincided with the eve of the feast of the Immaculate Conception, the commemoration in Catholic doctrine of the Virgin Mary's unique status in being born free from Original Sin (see 'Duns Scotus's Oxford', 1.14). Mary was thus conceived in order herself to conceive the holy body of Christ. Notions of conception and birth throes are here then extended to the nun's 'heart-throe' as, after hearing of ('conceiving') and carrying it, she finally gave birth to the word of God. Christ is thus both her 'lover' (st.25) and her husband. Nuns' habits, of course, are meant to represent them as brides of Christ.

Stanza 31

The nun becomes another Virgin Mary. Her pain in giving birth to God's word ('outright', st.30) finds reward in Christ who is now newly born to her (see st.34 and John, Ch.16, v. 21). Hopkins expresses his anguish, however, over those who have drowned as unbelievers or without absolution. Yet comfort, he imagines, can still be found in the hope that Providence may have used the nun as an agent of their salvation. Obedient to the 'Finger' of God's authority, as Hopkins himself in stanza one, the nun is imaged as a bell-wether, or leading sheep of a flock, which wears a bell and returns the sheep to the fold. There is evidence, too, that Hopkins may be referring to a then type of bell-buoy at sea known as a 'tall nun'. Changing the image again he now makes the storm into a winnowing wind separating out the chaff from the grain in God's harvest, and used in the memory of his own personal struggle with his God in 'Carrion Comfort' (ll. 7–9).

Stanza 32

At this point the poem moves into its final phase. God is addressed in terms of his strength and stolidity, 'recurb', 'wharf', 'Stanching', 'Ground', 'granite'. Just as in stanza one he is 'sway of the sea', here he becomes 'master of the tides', as indeed of all waters from the primeval Deluge ('Yore-flood') to the year's annual rainfall. Unlike the *Deutschland*'s master, whose incompetence ran the ship onto a sandbank, God shows a dependableness extending beyond his supervision of natural phenomena to a control even of our minds' unreliable variations. His unfathomable magnitude is acknowledged and his being is recognised as concealed, yet attentive, prescient, yet patiently awaiting the exercise of our free choice to serve him.

Stanza 33

As Noah's Ark rode out the waters of the 'Yore-flood', here God's mercy becomes an ark for the believer, with no limit placed on the extent to which it will try to find the not yet convinced or converted. Christ is a 'vein' through which prayers can be directed for those unable to pray for themselves (the Holy Souls in Purgatory) or who are in prison, or which can be accessed by the penitent on the very brink of death. Such represent 'the uttermost mark' of souls 'fetched' for himself by Christ who, like the victims of the *Deutschland*, 'plunged' into his own sufferings ('passion'), later to surface with his drowning people having saved them through his death and resurrection. He also takes on here the role of a benevolent 'giant' who 'strides' through this storm to the rescue. Hopkins indicates the scope of God's embracement by placing no syntactical break between this and the previous stanza and employing the same rhyme scheme in each – 'tides', 'sides', 'abides', 'outrides', 'glides', 'strides'.

Stanza 34

Through the nun's death Christ is 'new born'. He is both God and man ('double-natured') and described in a sequence of compound epithets: 'heaven-flung' (daringly, a kind of redemptive Satan!), a flame within the womb of Mary, and as the 'mid-numbered' or second person of the Holy Trinity. Hopkins sees Christ's presence in this shipwreck as a localized manifestation –'let flash to the shire' (Essex) – not as he once came ('dark') in the obscurity of his birth at Bethlehem, or as he will come again in power and majesty on the Day of Judgement. This particular coming is a gentle ('Kind') and propagating ('released shower') reclamation of his people.

Stanza 35

Hopkins prays to the nun, drowned on England's very doorstep, to remember its people now that in nautical terms she is in the 'roads', (a safe anchorage) and the 'haven' of her heavenly reward. He asks her to intercede with heaven's king to revisit his 'reign' (Catholicism) upon 'rare-dear Britain', a cry of characteristic exasperation with the country he so loves (cf. 'dear and dogged man' 'Ribblesdale'). There is also a sense of country in drought, needing 'rain' to make it flourish. 'Easter' is used as a verb with its sense both of resurrection and sunrise ('crimson-cresseted east'), and Hopkins concludes by inscaping the very being of his 'Lord', the final word of the poem, just as 'God' is the subject of its first line. Through a sequence of genitives he makes a closer and closer approach to the inner 'scape', the 'haecceitas' of Christ. Thus, the heart is centre of our being, charity the central virtue, the hearth (Latin -'focus') the centre of the house and the fire the centre of that hearth. Our 'heart's charity's hearth's fire', therefore, represents a deeply *heartfelt* focusing in upon Our Lord who is ultimately the source of all our most noble and chivalrous *thoughts*. Both heart and head together bring a highly wrought stanza and this most astonishing of poems to its conclusion.

3.2   Selected Poems

God's Grandeur:

A contrast is established between present ('now' ll.4/8) and past. Previous generations, through the immemorial processes of working lives lived out in natural surroundings, and who 'have trod' laboriously, have recognised God's grandeur in the world. The kinetic, electrical imagery which opens the sonnet suggests modern society in which God, although evident as ever, is now puzzlingly ignored (l.4). Where once earth's natural fruits such as (possibly implied here) olives for their oil, have been trodden for the precious exudation *expressed* from them, this world rightly seen is a similar ex-pression of God's grandeur. But a different oil ('smeared', 'smudge') now lubri-cates the machinery of 'toil' and 'trade'. The organic ('soil') has been replaced by the mechanisms of industry. Bare feet which once 'trod' are now 'shod' in boots. A work-force whose eyes are 'bleared' and 'bent' on profit as well as 'bent' over its toil has no opportunity to see what is so obvious in the grandeur of creation. Repetition of the conjunction 'and' in the octave suggests a relentlessness in nineteenth century human drudgery. Yet this same conjunction repeated in the sestet brings in a note of hope and regeneration (cf. its similar use in 'The Windhover' – 'AND the fire that breaks from thee then'). God persists in his creation in the form of the Holy Spirit who nurtures and revivifies. There are echoes of the Phoenix myth, the Book of Genesis (1, Ch.1, v.1–3) and *Paradise Lost* (1, ll.19–22). In 'Resolution and Independence' William Wordsworth's 'over his own sweet voice the Stock-dove broods' (l.5) anticipates the poet's own brooding anxieties in the subsequent narrative. 'Broods' may be being used by Hopkins in this sense of 'anxiety' (cf. 'this bids wear Earth brows of such care'; 'Ribblesdale'). The picture of a world spiritually rekindled has similarities with an apocalyptic vision of Wordsworth's in *The Prelude*:

> A thought is with me sometimes, and I say,
> Should earth by inward throes be wrench'd throughout,
> Or fire be sent from far to wither all
> Her pleasant habitations, and dry up
> Old Ocean in his bed left sing'd and bare,
> Yet would the living Presence still subsist
> Victorious; and composure would ensue,
> And kindlings like the morning, presage sure,
> Though slow, perhaps of a returning day[1]

For a more sceptical twentieth century view, Philip Larkin's 'Going Going' (*High Windows*, 1974) is worth consulting.

The Starlight Night:

The noun 'Starlight' lends a particularity to this night sky perhaps more effectively than the adjectival 'starlit'. Hopkins's idiosyncratic vision is similar in its way to that of Vincent Van Gogh's, in his painting, *The Starry Night* (1889). On two occasions, in lines eight and twelve, inner reflection replaces the outward-looking imperatives and imprecations as we are urged to look (seven times) at the sky and to 'bid' for and 'buy'

---

1   *The Prelude*, 1805, V, ll.28–36

its beauty. The process of imaginative creativity forms the constellations of stars into celestial townscapes ('boroughs', 'citadels', cf. Keats's imagined 'peaceful citadel' in 'Ode on a Grecian Urn') or wonderful faery worlds of diamond mines ('delves') and elves, bringing to mind Victorian conceptions of Shakespeare's *A Midsummer Night's Dream*, as in the strange, magical paintings of the Victorian artist, Richard Dadd .

More unusual analogies are made with natural things, 'lawns' (barren areas of sky), the movements of tremulous, silvery leaves on whitebeams and abeles (white poplars), and of snowflakes and startled doves. Like that of Keats in 'Fancy', Hopkins's imagination discards seasonal accuracies in order to put starry equivalents of March pussy-willow flowers and May blossom contemporaneously into various quarters of the sky. The 'starry' trees (for example, 'Look, look: a May-mess') take on the kind of visionary qualities associated with Samuel Palmer's representations of them in paintings such as *In a Shoreham Garden* (c.1829) or *The Magic Apple Tree* (1830). All this astonishing beauty is a 'purchase' because Christ has *redeemed* it; that is, he has *bought* it back (Latin 'emere' – to buy) from Satan; and we, too, can 'Buy' the 'prize', as at an auction, by bidding virtues and good works. In the imagery of Matthew, Ch.13, v. 30 we see a harvest-home with its bridegroom ('spouse') Christ, the Blessed Virgin and all the saints ('hallows'). The sky is the 'barn', or the 'paling' through whose fractures and crevices pieces of light, the 'piece-bright' stars, give us tantalising glimpses of the riches partly concealed from and awaiting us.

As Kingfishers Catch Fire

The poem acknowledges a Scotist 'haecceitas' or 'thisness' in everything. The main statement of the octave is 'each mortal thing does one thing and the same'. Preceding examples illustrate how this is true. Kingfishers with their iridescent plumage catch the fire of the sun; dragonflies 'draw flame' in their wake; stones which are tumbled over the rim of a well 'ring'. Hopkins uses a six word compound adjective to describe the noun, 'stones' – thus, what kind of stones? –'tumbled over rim in roundy wells' stones; musical strings and bells give out their individual personalities. Each thing 'selves' (Hopkins's own verb) and announces the particularity of its selfhood as the very reason for its being.

The sestet turns to a man who, in acting justly (he 'justices') reflects the infinite justice of Christ in whose image he is made. In consequence, he keeps God's grace as well as a gracefulness in everything he does. God the Father sees beauty in the eyes and limbs of just men who are themselves not Christ, but who are 'lovely' in feature to the Father as *reflections* of Christ. The contrast lies between 'each mortal thing', that is, each earthly thing which 'dies', and the infinite 'life' in God. The just man 'Acts' as Christ 'plays'. As Hopkins said in a sermon, 'It is as if a man said: "That is Christ playing at me and me playing at Christ, only that it is no play but *truth*";' (S 154, italics mine).   The prominent theatrical metaphor in the sonnet is used by Hopkins for the same purpose to which it is put in *Hamlet*. Hamlet distinguishes between playing (what 'seems') and what 'is': 'Seems, madam? Nay, it is. I know not "seems"'.[1] In Shakespeare's play, as in Hopkins's poem, however, acting or playing comes to be a way rather of revealing than of concealing the 'truth' – for Hamlet, that which 'is', for Hopkins, eternal life in God. The concept of 'truth' is similar in 'To what serves Mortal Beauty' where finite mortal beauty 'keeps warm/ Men's wits to the [eternal] things that *are*' (my italics).

Spring

The poem's time-honoured subject gains a new vitality in Hopkins's selection of details such as rampant weed growth rather than more conventional floral display. The omission of the definite article, [the] 'thrush/ Through the echoing timber' gives the birdsong an omnipresence, and it is as though heaven ('the descending blue') comes down to earth ('Thrush's eggs look little low heavens'). Hopkins sees spring as a 'strain', that is, a filtrate of, or perhaps a faint strain of music from, our lost Edenic condition. With characteristic urgency he commands Christ to claim for himself ('Have, get') the innocent May-time of as yet unspoiled youth, a time and condition most worthy of Christ's choice as, himself, the child of a 'virgin' mother. In a letter to Dixon Hopkins wrote that the 'Ode Intimations of Immortality from Recollections of Early Childhood' seemed to him 'better than anything else I know of Wordsworth's' (LD 148) and 'Spring' is his own version of it. The 'racing lambs' of line eight are likely to have been suggested by Wordsworth's line 'The young lambs bound/ As to the tabor's sound' quoted in Hopkins's journal entry of 1871 (J 206). Just as Wordsworth's 'Ode' as a whole regrets the 'earthly freight' of 'custom' descending on the 'growing boy' and dispersing the heaven which 'lies about us in our infancy', 'Spring' anticipates how the 'juice' of 'earth's sweet being in the beginning' is likely to 'cloy', 'cloud', and 'sour with sinning'.

The Sea and the Skylark

This sonnet regrets that man as 'life's pride and cared-for crown' should have lost his

---

1   *Hamlet*, 3. ii. 76

original happy condition and be put to shame by the simpler things of nature which 'ring out' his time as bells ring out the old year. The poem, written in the spring of 1877 like the previous ones above, intrudes a note of sadness into a generally happy and creative period for Hopkins. The sea's and skylark's 'noises' are so old as to seem almost timeless. The sound of the sea in the first quatrain, 'low lull-off or all roar' brings to mind the 'long, withdrawing roar' of the 'Sea of Faith' in Matthew Arnold's 'Dover Beach' (1867), a sound which 'Sophocles long ago' heard 'on the Aegean' and which, for Arnold, brings 'The eternal note of sadness in'. The 'old' noise of the skylark has similarities with the ancient song of Keats's nightingale whose voice was also heard by the sad-hearted Ruth in biblical times. At the same time, Hopkins's 'modern' imagination keeps in mind the scientific dependency of the sea's ebb and flow on the phases (the 'wear and wend') of the moon.

The second quatrain turns from the movement of the level sea to the vertical movement of the skylark, and in a letter to Bridges Hopkins explicated at length his intentions behind the complex phraseology describing the lark's impetuous and repeated outpourings. There is no need to assume that Hopkins singled out the little Welsh coastal resort of Rhyl, 'this shallow and frail town' and setting for the poem, for special criticism. Man's species ('make') and his creations ('making') are implicated only in his general sentiments. Both are 'breaking' and draining in a reversal of Darwinian evolutionary optimism towards 'dust' and 'slime'. Hopkins anticipates himself here in the last sentence of an undergraduate essay where he writes of the pre-Socratic Greek philosopher, Parmenides: 'Men , he thought, had sprung from slime' (J 130).

There is an undertow of world-sorrow in this sonnet which in some ways recalls the tragic register of Shakespeare's *Antony and Cleopatra*. Movement and flux are as central to that play as they are to this poem, and a line such as 'Frequenting there while moon shall wear and wend' captures something of the drama's authentic voice. Pulling in an opposite direction to Cleopatra's skylark-like airy aspirations is the Nile, with its muddy ('turbid') banks and the 'slime' of the 'aspic's trail' (V,ii,351–2). Perhaps it is significant that in a letter to Bridges Hopkins later recalled this poem to have been written in his 'salad days' (LB 163). The phrase is a direct echo of Cleopatra's words in 1.v.73.

In the Valley of the Elwy

The poet remembers a house in which he has spent a peaceful and hospitable episode. The occupants, who lived closely with nature, have come to represent for him a model of good society. There are similarities with this kind of natural domesticity in some of Coleridge's Conversation poems of the 1790's (for example, 'The Aeolian Harp', 'Reflections on Having Left a place of Retirement'). In recalling this house 'where all were good/ To me' Hopkins gives to nature the same moral values as Coleridge gives to it, and Wordsworth, too, in, for example, 'Tintern Abbey', where the 'forms of nature' are made responsible for his 'little, nameless, unremembered acts/ Of kindness and of love'. The restorative ('cordial'), sheltering ('hood') and protective ('mothering') environment was, to use Wordsworth's term, 'exquisitely fitted'[1] to the well-being of its inmates who, living in harmony with it, were being true to their own natures and therefore, inevitably, all seemed to be 'of course' and 'of right'.

In the sestet of the sonnet Hopkins turns to the beauty of the Welsh landscape but, this time, with a deep concern that here, unfortunately, 'the inmate does not correspond'. The poem concludes with his prayer that God, in his dual capacity as 'master'/'father' and 'fond'/'lover of souls' (cf. 'The Wreck of the Deutschland' l.71), will make good man's deficiencies through a process of balancing and regulating and bring him into a harmonious, moral relationship with his world.

The Windhover: *To Christ our Lord*

The Windhover is a kestrel, a small bird of prey that hovers stationary before swooping on its prey.

Hopkins frequently uses the verb 'to catch' when he refers to 'inscape': 'I caught an inscape as flowing and well marked almost as the frosting on glass and slabs' (J 227); 'I catch [...] the looped or forked wisp made by every big pebble the backwater runs over' (J 223). Here he remembers 'catching' (notice that the octave is in the past tense) a significant instant as if in a trap – 'sprung', like his own rhythm ('the word I use for this rhythm means something like *abrupt*', LD 23). Hopkins inscaped the hovering bird who rode the 'rolling level underneath him steady air'. Compare this lengthy compound adjective with the similar one in 'As kingfishers'). The bird's prominent exposure high in the air draws our attention, by contrast, to the obscurity of its admirer ('My heart in hiding'). The word 'Buckle', in the sestet, is the most notorious crux in the poem. In a journal entry for 12 July 1868 during his visit to Switzerland Hopkins, describing the dress of some local women, three times uses the word 'buckle(s)' to mean a fastening. Here it is likely that for a single moment all the qualities of the bird 'buckle!', or fasten together, as the full implication of that

---

1   Prospectus to *The Recluse*.

morning's experience is now understood and the inscape is 'caught' again. An analogy might be made with Wordsworth's concept of emotion recollected in tranquillity, as in 'Daffodils'– 'I gazed -and gazed- but little thought/What wealth the show to me had brought'. For Hopkins the wealth of this particular show is that, through his inscape of the windhover, he can now begin to imagine the 'billion/Times told lovelier, more dangerous' nature of God, as the capitalized 'AND' indicates.

The language of courtliness in this sonnet, the association of falconry with French chivalry and the bird as an heir apparent ('dauphin') who rides the air, all point 'to Christ our Lord' of the title, Hopkins's true 'chevalier'. 'The Windhover', like Blake's 'The Tyger', is a poem about creature and creator. Both creatures combine Burkean beauty and fear, and reflect the 'lovelier, more dangerous' nature of God.[1]

For Hopkins, God's glory is as much reflected in the 'sheer plod' of the lowly and humble ploughman's occupation (and by analogy, his own unsung, priestly profession) as in the obvious beauty of the falcon whose 'pride' and 'plume' possibly emphasise the dangers and vanities of worldly success. And this is no wonder, since the plough makes even a turned clod of clay 'Shine' (cf. the 'cold furls [...] shining', 'Harry Ploughman') and apparently dead, 'bleak' embers will fall to reveal the glowing fire within them.

At work within this sonnet are less obvious constructions and analogies. The poem encompasses the four elements of earth ('sillion'), air, water ('skate's heel') and 'fire'. It implies a diurnal cycle of temporal existence, 'dawn', 'morning', 'noon' ('High there') and evening ('embers'). And Christ's crucifixion, implicit in the words 'gall' and 'gash', ensures that the redemptive blood from the gashed body of the 'chevalier' (an appropriately royal colour, 'gold vermilion') and offered to all men, destroys invidious distinctions between the high-born and the lowly.

Pied Beauty

'Pied', meaning parti-coloured, is applicable to the 'skies' and 'finches wings'; 'dappled' is probably a more accurate descriptor for most of what else Hopkins here thinks of as reflecting God's nature. The title also encourages the reader to locate the beautiful in the unconventional. It has been pointed out that the opening , 'Glory be to God' and the ending, 'Praise him' are Latin 'A.M.D.G', 'A[d]. M[aiorem]. D[ei].

---

1   Edmund Burke, in *A Philosophical Enquiry into the Origin of our Ideas of the Sublime and the Beautiful* (1757), describes how the 'the strongest emotion the mind is capable of feeling' (the 'sublime'), is always accompanied by feelings of 'terror'; whereas those things perceived as 'beautiful' have qualities 'by which they cause love, or some passion similar to it'.

G[loriam]' and 'L.D.S', 'L[aus]. D[omino]. S[alvatori]' ('To the greater glory of God' and 'Praise be to Our Lord and Saviour') written at the beginning and end of all Jesuit works. As in 'The Windhover' the four elements are implicit: air ('skies'), water ('trout'), fire ('fresh firecoal chestnut falls') and earth ('plough'). The variegations extend from skies and landscapes, rivers and their contents, to different forms of trade and then to a variety of possibilities suggested by successive adjectives, some of which are contrastive. The poem acknowledges that disparate, changeable elements of creation are gathered into the unity of God who, 'past change' himself, is their self-begotten sire, 'All things [...] He fathers forth'. Hopkins employs a similar idea in 'To R.B.' where divine inspiration 'fathers thought' and leaves the poet's mind 'a mother of immortal song'. Coleridge defined the poet's creative imagination as 'a repetition in the finite mind of the eternal act of creation in the infinite I AM'.[1] The poet, he goes on to say, 'diffuses a [...] sprit of unity that blends, and [...] *fuses*, each into each, by that synthetic and magical power, to which we have exclusively appropriated the name of imagination.' In 'Pied Beauty' Hopkins sees God in creation as the supreme employer of that faculty which, as Coleridge writes:

> [...] reveals itself in the balance or reconciliation of opposite or discordant qualities: of sameness, with difference; of the general, with the concrete; the idea, with the image; the individual, with the representative [...] IMAGINATION [...] forms all into one graceful and intelligent whole.[2]

In this way the God of 'Pied Beauty' unites in himself the infinite varieties of the world which, like Coleridge's poet, he has 'imagined' into being.

The Caged Skylark

The diminutive skylark daringly confronts the 'gale' as the windhover 'Rebuffed the big wind'. Versions of freedom contrast with the incarceration of a wild bird in a cage and with man's spirit imprisoned within his 'Banhus' ('bone-house'), an Old English kenning for the body. The caged skylark which has forgotten its free fell country will still sometimes sing sweetly for a spell (a period of time), or sing magically. And likewise man, despite the daily drudgery of his working routine, has his intervals of pleasant respite. Hopkins himself as poet/singer may be implied here, as one who suffers his periods of dejection (an experience so much written about by the Romantic poets) in the course of his exhausting commitments as a religious. As

---

1   *Biographia Literaria*, Ch.13
2   *Biographia Literaria*, Ch.14

he does in 'God's Grandeur', and also to some extent in 'The Sea and the Skylark', Hopkins points up the nature of the Victorian work ethic. In line four, 'day-labouring-out life's age', he echoes Milton, 'Doth God exact day-labour…? (Sonnet: 'When I consider how my light is spent'), and brings to mind also his Samson, eyeless in Gaza at the mill with slaves, in *Samson Agonistes*. There is here, too, a suggestion of the bleak vision of Blake's industrial England with its 'dark Satanic Mills'. Inevitably in Hopkins's mind would be earlier literary skylarks – Shakespeare's lark 'at heaven's gate'[1], for example, and Shelley's skylark pouring its full heart 'from heaven or near it'.[2] 'The Caged Skylark' looks towards heaven at its conclusion by alluding to the Catholic doctrine of the resurrection of the body, in which it is taught that man will reassume his bodily condition but in a perfect form (Cor.1, Ch.15, v. 51-55) after death. An analogy is made between light meadow-down not being distressed by the 'weight' of a rainbow's foot, and man's resurrected body which will be, to his now 'uncumbered' self, as a 'wild nest' to a skylark – that is, no prison at all.

Hurrahing in Harvest

The title is a kind of cheer similar to 'my heart [...] would laugh, cheer' ('Carrion Comfort').The first quatrain presents a panoramic view of a wide harvest land and sky prospect. As stooks (sheaves of corn piled up to dry in the wind and sun) 'rise' in the fields the poet lifts 'up heart, eyes,/ Down', a strange construction reminiscent of Wordsworth's first view of an Alpine valley, 'My heart leap'd up when first I did look down', and both communicating a sense of rapture as the eye takes in huge vertical perspectives.[3] Here Hopkins can 'glean our Saviour' from the harvest setting in terms which recall the imagery at the end of 'The Starlight Night' (ll.12–13). His regret, too, that 'These things, these things were here and but the beholder/Wanting' compares with 'Only the inmate does not correspond' ('In the Valley of the Elwy'). What makes this particular sonnet so vivid is the erotic charge of the poet's reaction and the implications present in the physicality of his responses. The landscape becomes the body of Christ ('the azurous hung hills are his world-wielding shoulder'), and in the second quatrain he reaches and stretches to clasp his 'Saviour' in a recipro-cated embrace involving an erectile triplet, 'I walk, I lift up. I lift up heart, eyes' (cf. Edmund's rhythmically identical 'I grow, I prosper: Now, gods stand up'[4]) and com-

---

1   *Cymbeline*, 2, iii, 20
2   'To a Skylark'
3   *The Prelude*, 1805, VI, l.446
4   *King Lear*, 1, ii, 21–22

pounded by both the 'stallion' image in line ten, and 'The heart rears wings' in line thirteen. In a letter to Bridges Hopkins wrote:

> Feeling, love in particular, is the great moving power and spring of verse and the only person that I am in love with seldom, especially now, stirs my heart sensibly and when he does I cannot always 'make capital' of it, it would be sacrilege to do so' (LB 66).

Hopkins told Bridges that 'The Hurrahing Sonnet was the outcome of half an hour of extreme enthusiasm as I walked home alone one day from fishing in the Elwy'. (LB 56). The word 'Enthusiasm' possibly meant more here for the classicist, Hopkins, than it does for the general reader: in Greek, the word meant being possessed by, inspired by, the god ('en theos'). God becomes his intimate, and the moment of imagined congress produces an ecstasy which gets expressed in the breathless run of aspirants: 'And hurls for him, O half hurls earth for him' anticipated in the title. It is here that Hopkins comes close to the metaphysical poets in the intimate, daring manner in which he is sometimes capable of writing of his relationship with God.[1]

The Lantern out of Doors

The moving lantern evokes a passing interest; – 'who goes there?' is the challenge of a sentry. Where does the person come from, where is he bound as he goes 'down' the darkness as though through deep water with his 'wading light'? The second quatrain sees the lantern's progress through the dark as that of certain luminaries, beautiful in body ('mould') or in mind or in some other way, who illuminate our otherwise benighted lives for a while and are then themselves lost to our sight. The poet's wish would be to follow up their stories but, as he writes elsewhere, 'all is in an enormous dark drowned' ('That Nature is a Heraclitean Fire'). Unlike Christ he cannot 'be in at the end' of the story. The poem plays subtly with ideas of permanence and impermanence. The momentary and temporary diversion suggested by the phrase 'That interests our eyes' comes to be replaced by 'Christ's interest', his permanent and active concern through the duration of each life. The passing nature of all things, implicit in the commonly used phrase 'out of sight is out of mind', is replaced by the permanence of 'Christ minds'. Christ is the 'fast' (steadfast) friend – and here again the sentry's interrogation 'friend or foe' comes to mind. He is the alpha and omega ('first [...] last') of all existence who, having paid our ransom (bought us back), has rescued

---

1   See Hopkins's address to Christ, 'O my chevalier', 'ah my dear' ('The Windhover'): cf. Herbert: 'Ah my dear, I cannot look on thee' ('Love III'). And Donne: 'for I, /Except you enthrall mee, never shall be free,/ Nor ever chast, except you ravish mee' ('Holy Sonnet XIV').

us from our 'foe', our adversary, Satan, and from that 'death and darkness' which also had threatened to 'buy [us] quite'. The wandering syntax of 'wind/What most I may eye after' (that is, 'wind after with my eye what most I am straining to see') perfectly captures the movement of the lantern and probably derives from Imogen's account to Pisanio of how she would have gazed after the departing Posthumus:

> Thou shoulds't have made him
> As little as a crow, or less, ere left
> To after-eye him ...
> I would have broke mine eye-strings, crack'd them but
> To look upon him, till the diminution
> Of space had pointed him sharp as my needle;
> Nay, followed him till he had melted from
> The smallness of a gnat to air...[1]

Duns Scotus's Oxford

The opening inevitably invites comparison with Matthew Arnold's line from 'Thyrsis', written little more than a decade previously (1866), describing Oxford as 'that sweet city with her dreaming spires'. But Hopkins's run of compound adjectives energises the city where Arnold's elegy locates it sedately within a landscape of personal memory. The incursions of 'brickish' suburbs have upset that finely balanced ('poisèd') 'encounter' of nature with the graceful, ancient architecture of Oxford and disturbed the 'keeping', the special relationship, of 'folk, flocks, and flowers' in this peculiarly English version of pastoral. The same kind of intrusiveness can be found in Hardy's *Tess of the D'Urbervilles* (1891) where the D'Urberville mansion 'of the same rich red colour' as its 'crimson brick lodge' rises 'against the subdued colours' of the 'sylvan antiquity' of its setting (Chap. Five).

Wordsworth recalls of his student days in Cambridge, 'I could not print/Ground where the grass had yielded to the steps/Of generations of illustrious Men, /Unmov'd'.[2] At the beginning of the sestet Hopkins has similar thoughts about the presence in Oxford of the medieval scholar, Duns Scotus, whose philosophy was central to his own thinking and 'who of all men most sways my spirits to peace'. Of special concern to Hopkins with his devotion to the Blessed Virgin Mary, was Scotus's defence, in a public debate at Paris, of Catholic belief in the Immaculate Conception – in Mary, as

---

1   *Cymbeline*, 1, iii , 14–21
2   *The Prelude*, 1805, III, 261–4

mother of Christ, being uniquely free from original sin ('without spot'). Essentially, Scotus's philosophy was that God could be known through the senses and their experience of the individuality of 'each mortal thing' (see 'As kingfishers'), its 'haecceitas' (Latin: 'haec'/'this') or 'thisness'. The philosophy was at variance with that of St Thomas Aquinas, enshrined in Catholic doctrine, that knowledge of God could only be arrived at through a knowledge of universal things. Known as the 'subtle doctor' by tradition, Scotus seemed, to the Jesuit Hopkins, to sanction his own response to sensual appreciation of the real world of objects, 'of realty [reality] the rarest-veined unraveller.'

So, in a way, the very poem itself becomes a demonstration of Scotian belief. This is not Arnold's Oxford but Duns Scotus's Oxford, a lively and precisely individuated place, appealing not to a dreamy sense of the past but rather to the sight and hearing of its inhabitants, alert to all its wonderful detail and the 'goings on' of nature: 'Towery city and branchy between towers, / Cuckoo-echoing, bell-swarmèd, lark-charmèd, rook-racked, river-rounded'.

Binsey Poplars: Felled 1879

The poet feels personally bereaved by the destruction of the poplars which has been achieved with the ruthlessness of a military execution – of this particular 'rank', 'Not spared, not one'. The commemorative 'Felled 1879' is a kind of cenotaphic inscription because, after all, this has been a 'war' waged upon nature. The 'strokes of havoc' recall 'Cry "Havoc!" and let slip the dogs of war' (*Julius Caesar*, 3, i, 273). The leaves of the poplars had 'Quelled or quenched' the sun's heat. In a diary entry of 1864 Hopkins makes a reference, relevant to this image, to Shelley's: '"The Pine Grove near the Cascine" or something of the sort,[1] where the lines describing the twinkling of the sun through the leaves at morning occur' (J 19). Shelley's draft poem became 'To Jane: The Recollection' and contains lines referring to sunlight in leaves: 'And through the dark green crowd/The white sun twinkling like the dawn'. Its penultimate stanza contains a 'wandering wind' which 'Like an unwelcome thought [...] Blots thy bright image out'. Hopkins's comparatively early note seems to anticipate in Shelley's leaf-filtered sun and 'wandering wind' the 'wind-wandering' river bank of 'Binsey Poplars' as well as perhaps the stark 'death blots black out' ('That Nature is a Heraclitean Fire'). Christ's words on the cross, 'Father forgive them; for they know not what they do' (Luke, Ch. 23, v.34) are echoed in 'O if we but knew what we do/ When we delve or hew'. 'Delve' ('when Adam delved') reminds us of Christ

---

1   'The Pine Forest of the Cascine near Pisa'

as second Adam and, in this context, of fallen man's sacrilege against the fragility of the natural world. An analogy is drawn with the eyeball ('this sleek and seeing ball') whose ability to see is destroyed utterly by even the tiniest of injuries ('prick'). Implicit is Hopkins's anguish at man's inability to 'see' what lies plainly before him (cf. 'these things were here and but the beholder wanting'; 'Hurrahing in Harvest'). Even well meant interventions have a destructive finality, conveyed in the rhyme 'mend'/'end', and in the omission of the relative pronoun and auxiliary verb, 'beauty [that has] been'.

In 'As kingfishers' Hopkins writes of how each mortal thing 'selves'. The effect of the poplars' destruction has been to 'unselve' the 'especial' nature of the landscape where Hopkins is here using a particular Scotian phraseology. The triple repetition of 'rural scene', as in 'Rural rural keeping' ('Duns Scotus's Oxford') contributes a keening sound of regret for irreplaceable loss, as Milton makes repeated use of the open vowelled 'all our woe' to similar effect, reminding us of the consequences of Adam's fall in *Paradise Lost*.

Henry Purcell

Hopkins had a lifelong interest in music. He composed and was well-versed in musical notation. In a letter to Bridges he wrote: 'I am sometimes surprised at myself how slow and laborious a thing verse is to me when musical composition comes so easily (LB 136). In his undergraduate Platonic dialogue 'On the Origin of Beauty' he transfers to poetic composition the terms *diatonic* (parallelism, emphasis and intensity) and *chromatic* (tone and expression) (J 106). He will refer, for example to the 'Melodious lines of a cow's dewlap' (J 171), or a 'melodious' line of fir trees (J 172), to the 'slow tune' of the 'long shoulder' of Pendle Hill (J 205), and to chords, flats and sharps when describing the colour of Alpine lakes and the contours of mountainous topography (J 170). He would probably have sympathised with his Oxford tutor, Walter Pater's famous remark that 'all art constantly aspires towards the condition of music' and believed in the performative value of poetry which, he said, applied to all his verse.

Music which Hopkins particularly admired was that of the seventeenth century composer, Henry Purcell (1659–95) (LB 98). In this rather difficult Scotist sonnet he stresses not primarily what Purcell has in common with other composers, namely his ability to reflect our shared moods and emotions (ll.5–6), but rather, as his brief prose attachment acknowledges, Purcell's 'haecceitas', the 'rehearsal' or revelation of his 'arch-especial' selfhood which makes him peculiarly noted by Hopkins for 'the sakes of him'. By 'sakes', he wrote , 'I mean [...] the being a thing has outside itself [...] *and also* that in the thing by virtue of which especially it has this being abroad' (LB 83).

The poem begins with a past tense imperative (the construction being similar, as Hopkins explains, to '"Have done"' or '"Have had your dinner beforehand"' LB 174), commanding a fair fate to have fallen on Purcell since his death 'An age' since. Hopkins hopes, too, for a 'reversal' of his 'heresy', to a Catholic his Anglicanism, which 'here' (perhaps suggesting his tomb in Westminster Abbey) condemns him ('low lays him'), as well as suggesting his situation of being low-laid in that tomb. The beginning of the sestet asks Purcell's music to uplift the poet and, with a glance back at the low-laid composer, to 'lay me', that is, to charm and translate him with his musical 'air of angels'. There are puns on 'lay' as 'song' and 'air' as 'tune'. While the music plays, however, Hopkins remarks that it will not be Purcell's intentions he will 'Have an eye to' but rather what the composer, through his music, unwittingly communicates of his own 'abrupt self', the 'forgèd feature', by which he is known, as though he has been shaped or forged uniquely on an anvil. With a conceit almost as baroque as the music of Purcell itself, Hopkins compounds the idea by drawing an analogy with a 'stormfowl' which, intending flight ('meaning motion'), reveals in the rushing and displaying movements of its plumage as it lifts, an essential inner truth about its being, which produces wonder and surprise in the beholder. In the case of Purcell *and* the stormfowl 'each/Deals out that being indoors each one dwells' (see 'As kingfishers', 1.6, and cf. Hopkins's remark about 'sakes' above). This 'caught' moment of significance is reminiscent of 'The Windhover'. The 'colossal smile' of the bird's 'take-off' clearly refers to the markings of its feathers, but it also suggests something like an immensely pleasurable affirmation of the poet's own responsiveness to the 'divine genius of Purcell'.

The Candle Indoors

Though it was not originally intended, this poem, as Hopkins explained to Bridges, became a companion to 'The Lantern out of Doors' (LB 84). It is a reflective piece where the lack of specificity ('some candle...somewhere') and the poet's speculating intelligence transfers the interest away from the object to the state of his own soul. As he walks by the candlelit window, this time on the outside looking in (a reverse of his situation in 'The Lantern'), he hopes that whatever is going on by its light is being conducted to the greater glory of God. The candle's 'clear', 'blissful' and 'tender trambeams' are associated with the light of faith, with Christ as light of the world,[1]

---

1   William Holman Hunt's painting, *The Light of the World* (1851-53), at Keble College, Oxford, and

whose 'mild' authority puts gently but firmly back that 'blear-all black' implicitly threatening to blur the clearly drawn lines between moral good and evil.

Shakespeare's tragic hero, Macbeth, loses just this sense of these clear distinctions, reducing his 'single state of man' to one where everything becomes 'double', 'tedious' and life no more than a 'tale told by an idiot'. In the famous soliloquy, his exclamation 'out, out, brief candle' (5, v, 23) anticipates the darkness of his fate. Hopkins's poem also concerns itself with doubleness and duplicity. His advice to himself is to attend first to his *own* moral health – to avoid being the 'hypocrite', casting the mote from his neighbour's eye when all the while he has a 'beam' (using Christ's words as the basis for his pun) in his own: 'Thou hypocrite, first cast out the beam out of thine own eye; and then shalt thou see clearly to cast out the mote out of thy brother's eye' (Matthew, Ch.7, v.5). That the Greek word which gives us 'hypocrite' meant 'actor' (cf. 'I'll not play hypocrite/To own my heart'; 'Peace')[1] and therefore, by implication, 'liar', suggests that Hopkins may even have had Shakespeare's play in mind. Macbeth's 'candle' image gives way to his celebrated definition of man as an actor, 'a walking shadow, a poor player, /That struts and frets his hour upon the stage'. Hopkins poses his final question: 'Are you that liar?' – that is, an actor *pretending* to be the salt of the earth (Matt., 5.13) but, in fact, worthy only of being cast out by men of conscience as salt which has lost its savour.

Felix Randal

'Felix Randal' is based on Hopkins's experience as a parish priest at Leigh in the North west of England, and some of the Lancashire dialect finds its way into the poem, for example, the idiomatic 'and all' (l.6), 'all road' (l.8), 'fettle', (l.14). In the octave Hopkins records the demise of the strong blacksmith which he had observed in the course of his priestly visits to him. It begins conversationally with Hopkins receiving news of Felix's death, and leads to reflection on how the stricken and, at first, impatient farrier had 'mended' with the sacrament of Extreme Unction ('anointed'). This was a process begun 'some months earlier' when he had accepted Holy Communion, the body of Christ 'our sweet reprieve and ransom' (cf. 'ransom'; 'The Lantern out of Doors'), at Hopkins's hands. The verb 'tendered' as well as meaning 'given' suggests also the priest's tender approach to the sick man.

The first triplet of the sestet is Hopkins's implicit acknowledgement of his identification with Felix whose fate will ultimately be shared by all. The sentiments of

known to Hopkins can be found on the Web at http://www.etss.edu/hts/hts3/info17.htm
1   Phillips, p.149

line nine are identical with those of Wordsworth in 'The Old Cumberland Beggar', that sympathetic actions on behalf of those less fortunate not only assist the sufferer but also benefit the giver, 'That we have all of us one human heart' (l.146). Hopkins writes: 'This seeing the sick endears them to us, us too it endears...Thy tears had touched my heart […]'. The gentleness of speech ('tongue...taught') and 'touch' gives to Hopkins's ministry an irresistible Christ-like authority in contrast with the impatience and cursing of the once 'powerful' farrier. It is as though this unreflecting man had more in common with the brute creation ('Pining, pining' suggests an unhappy animal) and now, reduced to the condition of a little child ('child Felix'), he is under the stronger tutelage of God, his father.

The final triplet movingly imagines Felix Randal in his healthy years. The sense of line twelve is 'how far were you then, in all your more boisterous years, from thinking ahead to such times at these?' The last line of the sonnet, with its run of monosyllables, strikingly reproduces the blows of the blacksmith's hammer, and the use of the dialect word 'fettle' suggests a job completed once and for all (northern idiom: 'That's fettled him').

But the construction of the sonnet is interesting. We are made to encounter these vividly created sights and sounds only as we carry from the previous triplet the haunting knowledge of what is yet to come for 'poor Felix Randal'. The poem makes us reflect on one individual's death while reminding us that to each other we are all reminders of its inevitability.

Spring and Fall: *To a Young child*

The first line is a trochaic tetrameter, with two and a half stresses on 'Margaret' (not pronounced, 'Marg'ret').The name on which Hopkins places such a strong emphasis, means a 'pearl'. Pearls have traditional associations with tears, as they do, for example, in Richard Crashaw's poem about Mary Magdalene, 'The Weeper':

> When sorrow would be seen
> In her brightest majesty,
>   For she is a queen,
> Then is she drest by none but thee.
> Then, and only then, she wears
> Her richest pearls, I mean thy tears.

The tearful child, Margaret, grieves over the falling leaves of 'Goldengrove', a name which in this context has possible associations with Shakespeare's lyric in *Cymbeline* (see 'The Lantern out of Doors'), 'Golden lads and girls all must, /As chimney-sweepers, come to dust'.[1] The title points to our whole story of human experience with echoes, too, of Hopkins's own exhortation to Christ, the second Adam, to claim 'Mayday in girl and boy' ('Spring') before they suffer the inevitable consequences of the 'Fall'. Goldengrove may also point to the Golden Age, the classical version of Eden. The poet gently interrogates the grieving child, expressing mild surprise that she can show concern for the 'unleaving' grove with the 'fresh thoughts' of her tender years. The lines following on, in this poem which is addressed 'to a Young Child', recall Wordsworth's on the 'earthly freight' of 'custom' awaiting the 'little Child' of his 'Ode: Intimations of Immortality'. The mature heart, says Hopkins, will come 'colder' to such sights and spare (give) not even a sigh, 'And yet you *will* weep and know why'. Margaret is Hopkins's 'Weeper', too young to articulate what she instinctively feels (lines 12–13), 'the blight man was born for', but which she will inevitably come to 'know'. In words which echo Burns's lyric, 'Man was made to mourn', Hopkins tells the child, 'It is Margaret you mourn for'. He deploys a device usually reserved for conclusions in poetry, a triplet, in the middle of a poem otherwise written in couplets. The memorable middle line of the triplet with its long open vowels, 'worlds of wanwood', has the same aural effect as the opening 'Margaret' and the closing 'mourn' – a keening sound of regret, akin to Hopkins's use of the word, 'rural', in 'Duns Scotus's Oxford' and in 'Binsey Poplars'.

Inversnaid

'Inversnaid' was the product of a short excursion Hopkins made to Loch Lomond in the autumn of 1881. It describes the wildness of a landscape, a river and its waterfall, the identical setting of Wordsworth's 'To a Highland Girl (at Inversneyde, upon Loch Lomond' (1807). It is worth contrasting Wordsworth's briefest of references to 'This fall of water that doth make/A murmur near the silent lake' (ll.67–8) with the detail of Hopkins's powerfully realised scenery through which the river makes its headlong passage, like a horse galloping down a high road in a gothic verse-tale. There is an element of sublime fear in the deployment of words such as 'darksome', 'pitchblack', 'frowning', 'drowning' and, unlike Tennyson's fanciful brook which murmurs 'In brambly wildernesses',[2] the 'brook' of 'Inversnaid' 'treads' the 'groins of the braes' in this wild Scottish 'wilderness' rather as Coleridge's frightful fiend treads his 'lone-

---

1   *Cymbeline*, 4, ii, 262–3
2   Tennyson, 'The Brook'.

some road' in 'The Ancient Mariner' (ll.454–5). 'Inversnaid' shares with 'Binsey Poplars', 'Duns Scotus's Oxford', 'In the Valley of the Elwy' and 'Ribblesdale' a concern for the increasing threat to nature posed by the ruthless expansion of Victorian urban development, and Hopkins's own 'Despair' about the issue sits deeply at the heart of this poem.

Ribblesdale

Ribblesdale is where Hopkins spent periods of time at the Jesuit college of Stonyhurst in Lancashire. The River Ribble winds, as though from a 'reel' (l.7), through its beautiful dale. Hopkins's technique of 'vowelling off' – 'nay does now deal, /Thy lovely dale down thus and thus bids reel/Thy river', conveys a sense of the powerful hand of God displaying his 'sweet earth' as he spreads out the landscape before him. The simple leaves and grass 'with no tongue to plead' recall what Wordsworth describes as 'those unassuming things, that hold/ A silent station in this beauteous world' and which, by simply continuing to be, fulfil the intentions of their creator, appealing to him in their silent eloquence.[1] Since the Fall God no longer intervenes in his creation but freely 'gives o'er all to rack or wrong'. Earth's fortunes are now placed solely in the hands of man (ironically, 'life's pride and cared-for crown'; 'The Sea and the Skylark') who, in spite of all his superior endowments is obstinately ('dogged') in pursuit of whatever he is 'bent' on, tied to having his own 'turn' served first at whatever cost. In the process he gives no thought for the future of the world he will leave behind. The Earth which loves its 'dear' offspring (man) is therefore imaged as a fearful, anxious parent who, with 'brows of such care and dear concern', watches her child thoughtlessly plundering ('reave') and squandering a beautiful and irreplaceable inheritance, 'heir' only to its own uncaring selfishness.

To seem the stranger

In the first quatrain the poet presents himself as a stranger among his fellow men, not only as an Englishman among the Irish, but also by nature of his temperament and vision. He feels the pain of being apart from his family who, as members of the Anglican community, are estranged from his own profound commitment to the Catholic faith. Also, there is his sense that Christ, the reason for his 'parting' and his means to true peace, appears to be the source of his deepest anguish ('sword and strife'). The oblique in 'my peace/my parting' accentuates this apparent irreconcil-

---

1   *The Prelude*, 1805, XII, ll.51–2

ability. Christ's radical words themselves promise such difficulties: 'Think not that I am come to send peace on earth: I came not to send peace, but a sword. For I am come to set a man at variance against his father, and the daughter against her mother' (Matthew, Ch. 10, v. 34–5). Hopkins in these sonnets, however, never questions God's wisdom. He only sometimes registers his bafflement, as to *seem* estranged from Christ does not necessarily mean to be so.

The second quatrain turns from familial and spiritual issues to those associated with creativity and politics. Hopkins, as an ardent patriot, found himself in a Jesuit community in Dublin where there was active support for Irish home rule. Though not unsympathetic to it, he found himself in the same kind of moral dilemma as that remembered of his youthful self by Wordsworth in *The Prelude*. Wordsworth's 'conflict of sensations without name' came about through his inability to reconcile his love for his native country with his French republican sentiments, so that at church, when prayers were being said for England's military victory over France, he describes how 'I only, like an uninvited Guest/Whom no one own'd sate silent'.[1] Hopkins expresses his helplessness ('idle a being') in this arena of political attrition while the enjambed 'wear-/Y' implies a sense of the situation's endlessness. England, too, he describes as 'wife/To my creating thought'. To Bridges he wrote: 'A great work by an Englishman is like a great battle won by England' (LB 231), but his own attempts at publication had been met with rejection. England, he feels, would turn a deaf ear to his pleas, even were he to make them.

Hopkins's notion of England as wife to his muse has similarities with Keats's imagery in his sonnet 'On Sitting Down to Read "King Lear" Once Again' where Shakespeare is presented as 'begetter' of his drama on the 'clouds of Albion'. Keats, who aspires to a comparable creativity, pleads not to be left to 'wander in a barren dream'. Issues of poetic barrenness and fertility are also very much in Hopkins's thoughts in the celebrated phrase, 'Time's eunuch' ('Justus quidem tu es, Domine') and in the imagery of his sonnet, 'To R.B'.

The poet describes himself as being at 'a third/Remove', possibly thinking of his situation first as a Catholic priest estranged from his family, secondly of being accepted as a creative artist and published poet and, finally, as separated geographically from his own country. There is no real impediment, as he acknowledges, either to giving love or receiving it from others; his sense of being a stranger has deeper causes which, either for good or ill, thwart whatever expression of his inner wisdom needs to be given. To 'hoard' his wisest 'word' (perhaps here specifically his poetry)

---

1   *The Prelude*, 1805, X, II.266–75

recalls an Anglo-Saxon poet's 'word-hoard'. But Hopkins is unheard and, if heard at all, neglected, suggesting an almost intolerable tension between the chosen renunciation of his gifts and the desire to be recognised and accepted for them. The shrunken voice of the final phrase 'leaves me a lonely began' creates a sense of his being left behind in the distance, like a promising racehorse which, although it began its race, has been pulled up and has failed to run the course.

I wake and feel

Waking into darkness the poet reflects on the horrors he has encountered in sleep. He refers to his heart as a 'witness' to the sights he saw and ways he went, as though his heart has been a fellow-traveller on some infernal journey not yet concluded ('And more must, in yet longer light's delay'). The experience of what is only a matter of hours has seemed more like 'years' or a whole lifetime, and his cries to God for relief are like so many 'dead letters' which have been sent to the wrong address.

Without an assurance of God, his life becomes an intolerable solitude. His sense of himself as a living embodiment of distasteful physical disorders reminds him that, by his very existence ('Bones...flesh...blood'), he inherits the primal 'curse' and that he shares in the suffering which Christ himself endured to abolish it. 'God also committed Christ, his son, to the loneliness, the bitterness of the 'gall' (l.9) and the 'scourge' (l.13) of his passion and death. And in this fundamental sense the poet is not, in fact, alone but at one with his God, even though his present experience is of himself as a contaminated yeast which 'sours' the bread of life. If there is any consolation for him in this dark night of the soul it is that, although he suffers dreadfully, there is still, at least for him, the possibility of redemption. For the 'lost' the situation is 'worse' in that *their* sufferings will be endless.

'I wake and feel' gives a very tactile sense of spiritual darkness. The 'fell of dark' recalls Macbeth's 'fell of hair' (5, v, 11) and the 'blanket of the dark' (1, v, 53) points us to a similarity in both protagonists. In Hopkins's sonnet the emphasis is on the personal pronoun, 'I', (used eight times) and on other pronouns 'you', 'we', 'my', 'me', 'mine', all of which refer the situation to himself. Macbeth's sense of being isolated ('cabin'd, cribb'd, confin'd' 3, iv, 23) by an act through which he has murdered sleep (I, ii, 33) causes him to try to escape self by realising an objectivity in a tactile world beyond the self –'Strange things I have in head, that will to hand' (3, iv, 129); 'The very firstlings of my heart shall be/The firstlings of my hand' (4, i, 147–8). Hopkins's sonnet, too, shares common ground with Coleridge's 'The Pains of Sleep' in which nightmares of 'loathing', 'remorse' and 'woe' are a source of horror and anguish. At the same time, however, Hopkins is free from Coleridge's self-regarding insistence on an explanation for his sufferings, 'wherefore, wherefore fall on me?' (1.50). Even in extremity Hopkins is never recalcitrant. He accepts from 'dearest him' that 'deep decree' as something unfathomable yet, nevertheless, obligatory.

'No Worst'

The first statement seems to owe something to Edgar's remark in *King Lear*, 'the worst is not/So long as we can say, "This is the worst"' (4, i, 28–9). Here 'more pangs' instructed or 'schooled' by previous ones are likely to produce worse. Belial's remarks to Moloch, in *Paradise Lost*, that a much worse situation could well replace their current unenviable predicament as fallen angels make another possible contribution to the sonnet: 'Is this then worst, /Thus sitting, thus consulting, thus in arms?' (1,163–4). Like 'fell' in 'To seem the stranger', 'pitched'/'pitch' are words capable of carrying several meanings, for example, 'thrown', 'black bitumen', 'height', 'tuned'. The poet calls on the Holy Ghost and the Virgin Mary for comfort. The countless cries of his lament in 'I wake and feel' become here 'herds long', heaving and restless like a slow-moving drove of lowing cattle. He huddles for refuge in the midst of not just a personal 'woe' but a 'world-sorrow', a misfortune visited upon the whole of mankind in general as a result of the Fall. Yet, in spite of suffering painful blows upon this 'age-old anvil', the true Christian, because of his assurance of redemption, can still 'sing' in his anguish. There are momentary lulls in the poet's ordeal only to be replaced by Fury's ruthless determination to deal summarily with him ('No ling-/Ering' cf. 'Wear-/Y; 'To seem the stranger').

The sestet's memorable image of a vertiginous precipice over which the victim may topple into an abyss of mental catastrophe recalls Wordsworth's lines in the 'Prospectus' to 'The Recluse'. In broadening his theme beyond that of *Paradise Lost* and no doubt recalling Satan's fall to 'bottomless perdition' (1, 47) Wordsworth writes:

> Not chaos, not
> The darkest pit of lowest Erebus,
> Nor ought of blinder vacancy – scooped out
> By help of dreams, can breed such fear and awe
> As fall upon us often when we look
> Into our Minds, into the Mind of Man [...]

For true understanding Hopkins emphasises the necessity of experience. Those who have never 'hung' there may well underestimate the terror. He advises himself to take the kind of qualified shelter to be found in the eye of a storm ('under a comfort serves in a whirlwind'), consoling himself that as 'each day dies with sleep' death brings an end to all life and suffering, and then even our 'small/Durance' (endurance) will no longer be called upon. An echo of *Lear* would seem to end as it begins this sonnet, in the King's advice to his Fool to enter a hovel, to huddle and shelter from the storm: 'Nay, get thee in: I'll pray, and then I'll sleep' (3, iv, 26–7).

To what serves Mortal Beauty?

Mortal beauty refers here not simply to physical, human beauty, but to a beauty which as potentially the cause of '*mortal* sin' would deprive the soul of sanctifying grace. To the Catholic Hopkins this meant the soul's death and its eternal damnation. Beauty is 'dangerous' in its arousal of emotions which can lead to such sin. Interestingly, though, the answer the poet provides to his own question begins in the middle of the third line – 'See: it does this:' – preceding it, is his reflective dalliance with that very beauty whose danger is being acknowledged; as if the first sentence itself is demonstrating how alluring and distracting the power of beauty can be.

The transient beauty of a face (inviting our instinct to 'seal' it from vanishing away) 'does set danc/Ing blood'. The enjambed line 'dancing' into the next one imagines beauty's self as a 'flung prouder form' than that of someone *actually* dancing to a tune by Henry Purcell – for Hopkins a very visible manifestation of 'abrupt self' ('Henry Purcell', l.8). Beauty as a 'proud' form here further compounds the idea of the sinful possibilities associated with it.

The answer to the initial question resumes (l.3), but is again, revealingly, almost immediately replaced by the poet's further reflections on how a glance from a beautiful face can 'master' more than a 'gaze'. A gaze, being a too obviously intimate encounter, is in danger of discountenancing both persons involved. The implicit brevity of 'glance' is taken up by the rhyming 'that day's dear *chance*' (italics mine) which refers to a chance meeting of Pope Gregory with 'Those lovely lads' from Britain being sold as slaves in a Roman marketplace. Their beauty, according to the story, attracted his attention (allegedly he remarked 'Non Angli, sed angeli' ('Not Angles, but angels')) which had important consequences in that it was the reason for the Pope's despatching Augustine to introduce Christianity to Britain. Here the power of physical beauty occasioned the conversion of an entire nation from the worship of 'block or barren stone' to the truth of Christ. Christianity's ('our law['s]') own view of beauty, says Hopkins, is that, when met with, it should simply be inwardly acknowledged ('own/Home at heart') as 'heaven's sweet gift', but then 'let...alone'. Love should be directed rather at one's fellow men, at what is expressed of their inner selfhood in all its individual manifestations. Physical beauty may be one means of our accessing God, but it is better to wish a beautiful person, as indeed, all men, 'God's better beauty, grace'.

A letter to Bridges, about five years before this sonnet was written, contains Hopkins's thoughts on different forms of beauty which have relevance for this poem:

> I think then no one can admire beauty of the body more than I do, and it is of course a comfort to find beauty in a friend or a friend in beauty. But this kind of beauty is dangerous. Then comes the beauty of the mind, such as genius, and this is greater than the beauty of the body and not to call dangerous. And more beautiful than the beauty of the mind is beauty of character, the 'hand-some heart'[1] (LB 95)

'To what serves Mortal Beauty'?, however, seems to reveal (as in 'To seem the stranger') yet another tension in Hopkins between his professed rejection of earthly ties as a priest, who has vows of poverty, chastity, obedience, and the intensity of his love for all earthly beauty.

(Carrion Comfort)

The use of 'Not' four times in the twelve opening words, makes a powerful state-ment of the poet's determination to resist temptation. To abandon responsibility for one's actions because of a conviction that there is no hope ('de-sperare', from hope), although it might bring the apparent comfort of release from all moral exertion, would in reality be like feasting on dead and putrefying flesh. In Catholic doctrine Despair, together with Presumption, is one of the two sins against the Holy Ghost; to despair of being saved, or equally, to presume salvation; hence the strength of Hopkins's resistance to such illusory 'comfort'. The relatively weak struggles he is still able to make, however ('me [...] not weary'), can only be expressed in negative terms reflect-ing the situation to which he has been reduced. He can still, as he says, 'not choose not to be'.

The second quatrain typically questions God's purpose with four interrogatives imaging God as a force which treads on him ('why do you rudely rock your earth-

---

1   See 'The Handsome Heart', Phillips, p.144

shaking foot on me?') or as a carnivorous beast preparing to devour, as it breathes and gazes on him. The poet as 'frantic to avoid thee and flee' recalls the actions of those who will witness Christ's second coming: 'Then let them which be in Judaea flee into the mountains' (Matthew, Ch. 24, v. 16). The sestet goes on to anticipate the Last Judgement, using John the Baptist's imagery which speaks of Christ as one 'Whose fan is in his hand', and who will 'thoroughly purge his floor, and gather his wheat into the garner' but who will 'burn up the chaff with unquenchable fire' (Matthew, Ch. 3, v. 12). Hopkins supplies his own answer to his previous questions when he is able to understand that God's punitive 'tempest' is simply the 'fan' to separate out the poet's 'chaff' from his 'grain'.

That God has all along been the author of this salutary tempest recalls how, in Shakespeare's *The Tempest*, Prospero, too, as author of an apparently destructive storm, brings joy out of despair. Alonso, King of Naples, who 'receives [*true*] comfort like cold porridge' (2, i, 10), feasts on the 'comfort' of despair because he thinks he has no hope of ever again seeing his son, Ferdinand. Prospero's transformation of such hopelessness and loss is preceded by a mask in which he displays his authority in terms of fruitfulness and harvest (4, i, 111/114–5). In 'The Wreck of the Deutschland' Hopkins (using *The Tempest*'s form of the word 'wreck') asks 'is the shipwrack then a harvest, does tempest carry the grain for thee'? (st.31). Prospero's symbol of power is his staff, and it is God's 'rod' which Hopkins learns here to 'kiss'. Divine benevolence entices the poet back from his flight as a panic-stricken animal to what we imagine of that animal making its first tentative re-approach, lapping strength, stealthily taking joy and then gradually building in confidence ('laugh, cheer'). Clearly the poet's ordeal has now passed but he is left in an emergent state of uncertainty, bewildered as to what it is he should rightly be celebrating. In a scene which recalls the biblical Jacob wrestling with the angel (Genesis, Ch. 32, v. 24-5), Hopkins, in the parenthetical exclamation ('my God!'), makes a common expression register equally the shock of his recognition that his supposed adversary was in fact his Saviour: 'That night, that year/Of now done darkness' may refer to a protracted period of time or, as in 'I wake and feel', to what had been imagined as years being in fact no more than a few hours of intense suffering.

Patience, hard thing

'The virtue of the soul that is called patience', wrote St Augustine, 'is so great a gift of God, that we even plead the patience of Him who bestows it upon us'.[1] Hopkins's

---

1   *The Catholic Encyclopedia*, online

opening remark implies that although it is easy to pray for the relief of our suffer-ings it is much more of a 'hard thing' to pray for the patience to bear them. To do so seems to invite, unquestioningly, strife, anguish, and endless renunciation. Yet 'Rare patience' is something not simply to pray for but, because of its rarity, to make 'bid for' as a 'prize' (cf. 'Buy then! Bid then! -What? – Prayer, patience, alms, vows'; 'The Starlight Night'). Patience can only reveal its existence as a virtue where suf-fering requires it to be exercised (l.15), and in a complex metaphor Hopkins images what he calls 'Our ruins of wrecked past purpose' as a crumbling edifice masked by patience, the 'ivy' of the heart.

The 'liquid leaves' of the ivy whose 'purple' berries 'bask' in its deep green 'seas' also make 'Our [...] wrecked past purpose' into a shipwreck; compare Hopkins's own sense of himself as a 'foundering deck' in 'That Nature is a Heraclitean Fire' (l.18). In the first triplet of the sestet Hopkins concedes that despite the almost unbearable situ-ation of inviting more affliction, he nevertheless considers it appropriate to ask God to 'bend to him' his 'rebellious will'. The language recalls John Donne's 'bend/Your force, to break, blowe, burn and make me new'.[1] The violence is succeeded by a more gentle register. Hopkins is still searching for an apparently absent God ('where is he') but imagines him, the model of this virtue, as a bee filling his combs with the honey of Patience, and drawn perhaps from the poisonous ivy flower, a distillation of delicious sweetness, just as the sweet virtue itself is here, of course, drawn from the toxin of suf-fering. Hopkins may have had in mind Keats whose sweet pleasure in Melancholy is in the very process of 'Turning to poison while the bee-mouth sips'.[2] In 'Isabella' Keats writes: 'Even bees, the little almsmen of spring-bowers, /Know there is richest juice in poison flowers'. Hopkins's sonnet ends with his acknowledgement that the sweetness of patience comes to us only through those ways which we know to be difficult.

My own heart

Hopkins advises himself to show some charity (St Paul's greatest virtue, 1 Cor., Ch.13, v.13) to his own heart. His mind is depicted as a relentless self- torturer and he urges it to relent and have 'pity' on itself. The poet has reached an impasse in his sufferings where he is no more capable of alleviating them than a blind man can find sight by groping for it, or 'thirst' in 'a world of wet' can truly know the complete fulfilment of quenching itself. In the first triplet of the sestet Hopkins advises his 'jaded', humdrum self ('Jackself') to 'call off thoughts awhile', as if his overactive scruples were dogs

---

1   John Donne, 'Holy Sonnet XIV'
2   'Ode on Melancholy'

endlessly worrying at or savaging him. Comfort is a plant which needs space to root and grow ('size') towards proper establishment. Hopkins skilfully uses two colloquial expressions (cf. ('my God!'); 'Carrion Comfort'), 'God knows when' and 'God knows what', which have an immediate sense of bewildered incomprehension, but the profounder one of it being indeed God who truly *does* know these things. God's kindness cannot be forced from him (the continuation of 'smile/'s' from line twelve into line thirteen communicates this idea), coming rather at 'unforeseen times' when it is not expected and when the intensity of self-examination has slackened and created more appropriate conditions for it. Hopkins's analogy is with a track of light seen through, and extending beyond, a cleft in a mountain range. His coined verb, 'to betweenpie', implies that skies create a dappled effect (cf. 'Pied Beauty'). They 'Betweenpie mountains' and light 'a lovely mile' stretching visibly ahead through the dark terrain.

Spelt from Sibyl's Leaves

This sonnet takes its title from the Cumaean Sibyl. In Roman myth she was a prophetess who foretold events by writing her prophecies on leaves which the wind then blew haphazardly about. The 'Dies Irae' in the liturgy of the Catholic Church's Requiem refers both to King David and to the Sibyl as foretelling the dissolution of the world at the Last Judgment. Hopkins sees in the onset of evening a prophetic warning of that final reckoning ('Heart you round [warn] me right with'). As the variegated colours of daylight resolve themselves ('her dapple is at end') into monochromatic 'black, white', so too will God's judgement only concern itself with matters of 'right, wrong', moral good and evil. Evening, therefore, becomes an admonition, ('Our tale, O our oracle!) advising us to be 'ware of' ('beware of' or be 'wary of'), to reckon seriously with ('reck but'), a world where ultimately only these two issues will matter.

There is something very sombre in the steady advance of the first line where seven sonorous adjectives define night's inevitable approach. Its immensity seems to include the whole cycle of earthly existence, 'womb-of-all, home-of-all, hearse-of-all'. The rays of the setting sun, 'Her fond yellow hornlight', are replaced by an afterglow (cf. 'the sun put out his shaded horns very clearly and a longish way. Level curds and whey sky after sunset', J 141–2) amidst which the stars in their various magnitudes become systematically visible, 'earliest stars, earl stars, stars principal' (cf. 'A star most spiritual, principal, pre-eminent/Of all the golden press', J 50). These stars, however, are not the delightful 'fire-folk sitting in the air!' of 'The Starlight Night', but stars which have an ominous authority over our fates ('overbend us'), boding our imminent judgement as in Matthew's Gospel, 'the stars shall fall from heaven [...]

and they shall see the son of man coming [...] with power and great glory' (Matthew, Ch. 24, v. 29–30). Against the remaining faint, bleak light of the sky the black leaves of the 'dragonish' trees appear beaked, with almost a Disney-like animation, and their boughs on such a 'tool-smooth' background are like the filigree tracery of damascene work on a sword blade (cf. 'tool' for 'sword'; *Romeo and Juliet*, 1, i, 31).

Gradually, the individuality of all created things is lost as, with the approach of night, clearly defined boundaries are eroded and merged – the syntax and rhythm contributing to the sense of universal dissolution: 'as-/Tray or aswarm, all throughther, in throngs; self in self steeped and pashed – quite/Disremembering, dismembering all now'. A twentieth century poem, the brief 'Days' by Philip Larkin, addresses, like Hopkins (though without any assurance of a deity), the stark realities posed by the question, 'Where can we live but days?' In 'solving that question', and with no more days to follow, black and white figures (priest and doctor) are brought 'In their long coats/Running over the fields'.[1] 'Spelt from Sibyl's Leaves' envisages the separation of everyone at judgement, as sheep from goats (Matthew, Ch. 25, v. 31–3), 'part, pen, pack/ Now her all in two flocks, two folds'. To be at that time on God's left hand will be to 'go away into everlasting punishment' (Matthew, Ch. 25, v. 46), to experience the horror of self-responsibility for eternal loss, where 'selfwrung, selfstrung, sheathe – and shelterless, thoughts against thoughts in groans grind'. Although not specifically of the group of desolation sonnets, this poem shares its sentiments with those of 'I wake and feel' (ll.9–14) and 'Patience, hard thing' (ll. 9–10).

Harry Ploughman

Hopkins wrote to Bridges: 'I want Harry Ploughman to be a vivid figure before the mind's eye; if he is not that the sonnet fails' (LB 265). The occasional obscurity of Hopkins's style is evident in this poem, although it is not essentially any more difficult than in others. Critical assessments have tended to balk at the use of certain words, 'flue', 'quail', 'frowning', for example, which Hopkins obviously chooses to use in a particular way, but otherwise the meaning is reasonably clear. The octave is a strongly visualised presentation of Harry's physique. His body is depersonalized and anatomically interesting. He is a static figure made vivid, as Hopkins wished, in the same way as Wordsworth's 'Solitary Reaper' ('Behold her, single in the field') or the old leech gatherer of 'Resolution and Independence'. Just as the leech gatherer is compared to a 'huge stone' or a 'Sea-beast', Harry's arms are 'Hard as hurdle' (twisted willow twigs), his limbs 'as a beechbole firm'. Harry commands each part of his body

---

1   *The Whitsun Weddings*, 1964

as though he were the captain and his various members a ship's crew. All 'fall to' and await his orders to action. Each limb and part expresses ('features, in flesh') what it is designed to do. The effect is rather like that of a freeze-frame in cinema, where the tension ('Stand at stress') gets resolved as the film is allowed to roll. This happens in the first line of the sestet when Harry suddenly begins to move, 'He leans to it, Harry bends, look'. What is depicted resembles early footage where the dynamics of human or animal movement can be revealed and slowly and objectively examined.

Nothing more is known about Harry's life except that his profession is that of ploughman (cf. Welsh usage, 'Jones the Baker'). Much less an individual than Felix Randal he is representative only of universal male power, 'child of Amansstrength', where the capitalisation and compound form lend a mythic quality to his forbear. In the last sentence of the sestet Hopkins attempts to convey lexically a synonymity of movement and action which is cinematic in effect. The sense is 'Churlsgrace [the grace of a peasant]...hurls/Them [the turned clods of earth].../ With-a-fountain's shining-shot-furls'. But to convey the movement of Harry as he ploughs, an entire clause is incorporated within the dashes: '– broad in bluff hide his frowning feet lashed! Raced/With, along them, cragiron under and cold furls' –.

Such innovative writing is not peculiar to this poem. Hopkins aims for a similar effect in 'The Wreck of the Deutschland': 'They fought with God's cold – / And they could not and fell to the deck/ (Crushed them) or water (and drowned them) or rolled/ With the sea-romp over the wreck' (st.17). Hopkins was himself dubious about what he was attempting in 'Harry Ploughman': 'The difficulties are of syntax no doubt. Dividing a compound word by a clause sandwiched into it was a desperate deed, I feel, and I do not feel that it was an unquestionable success' (LB 265). Nevertheless 'the fascination of what's difficult', in W. B. Yeats's phrase, drove him constantly to attempt to take the possibilities of language into new territory. Modernist prose writers such as Conrad and Joyce have close affinities with what would become common cinematic technique, and in 'Harry Ploughman' Hopkins, too, seems definitely to be pointing poetry in that direction.

Tom's Garland: *Upon the unemployed*

Like 'Harry Ploughman', this poem is about an individual seen as representative type. Just as the ploughman's several bodily parts make up the perfectly functioning workman, Tom is part of a commonwealth which operates as a human body, the monarch as 'lordly head,/With heaven's lights hung round', Tom as its 'mighty foot' which 'mammocks' or disfigures (as Hopkins said, by trenching, tunnelling, blasting LB

273) its 'mother ground'. Tom, as the foot of society, is given prominence from the start with the emphasis placed on his workman's boots whose soles are 'garlanded' with 'surly steel' nails. There is something witty and sportive here, similar in its way to Shakespeare's inversion of order in *A Midsummer Night's Dream*, which can sometimes apotheosise Bottom, the bottom of society, at the expense of Duke Theseus at its top. At the end of his day's labour Tom downs tools ('piles pick') and heads for home, supper and bed alongside his fellow workman ('fallowbootfellow') 'sturdy Dick'; fallow because at rest and no longer at work. His steel-nailed boots make sparks on the ground ('rips out rockfire') as he walks. The contrast is perhaps with Hopkins himself whose life with 'Thousands of thorns, thoughts' could not be more remote from that of Tom who, 'prickproof', enjoys, like Larkin's 'Old Prijck', the 'secret bestial peace' of the carefree lowly.[1] In lines 8–10 Tom's thoughts are imagined as he voices acceptance of his lot, his patriotic fervour and an acknowledgement that he would probably be at the bottom of the pile ('lacklevel in') even were wealth to be more equally distributed.

Hopkins then turns to different members of society, the disinherited ('Undenizened') who are excluded both from 'earth's glory' and 'earth's ease', who have no identity within it ('no-one, nowhere') and, devoid of the comforts of the top and bottom strata, ('rare gold, bold steel, bare /In both') share only the 'care' of each. To the conservative Hopkins the danger would appear to be that such conditions produce either the apathy of 'Despair', breeding sullen, disaffected people, or what for him would seem to be much 'worse', the 'Rage' which is the source of mob violence. Fear of the mob, something he shared with many of his Victorian contemporaries, is expressed in words such as 'Manwolf' and 'packs' suggesting that he considers the unemployed as potentially predatory animals to be eradicated from a country they 'infest'.

Earlier in the poem Hopkins sees no way in which the 'unemployed' can be 'sped' either by the mental or physical options ('mind nor mainstrength') available to them through the commonwealth. To Bridges he had written, 'And this state of things, I say, is the origin of Loafers, Tramps, Cornerboys, Roughs, Socialists and other pests of society' (LB 274). Lines 13–14 express both his preference for those working men who are content to 'plod safe shod sound' and his anxiety about the instincts of Socialists to reward the dispossessed, exposing them to the dangers of undeserved and unearned wealth ('gold go garlanded/With, perilous, O no';).

---

1   'The Card Players', *High Windows*, 1974

In 1865 Hopkins had visited Ford Madox Brown's exhibition in Piccadilly and had seen his celebrated painting, *Work*.[1] He had copied Brown's accompanying <u>sonnet</u> into his commonplace book and the ethos of both painting and sonnet underlie 'Tom's Garland'. Both reflect the Victorian work ethic, memorably articulated in Thomas Carlyle's *Past and Present* (1843) – 'Think it not thy business, this of knowing thyself [...] know what thou canst work at; and work at it, like a Hercules'. However, the reactionary and anxious register of this poem does not cleanly represent Hopkins's thoughts about the underprivileged. A breach in the friendship between himself and Bridges, lasting for two and more years, was caused by Hopkins's so-called <u>'red letter'</u> in which he startlingly confessed, 'Horrible to say, in a manner I am a Communist' and expressed his understanding of the alienation of whole sections of society unable to share in the prosperity they were responsible for creating (LB 27–8).

Perhaps even more so than 'Harry Ploughman' 'Tom's Garland' represents Hopkins's poetry at its most obscure. In a letter to Bridges of 1888 Hopkins provided a useful 'crib' in response to the complaints of both Bridges and Canon Dixon that they were defeated by this poem: 'O, once explained, how clear it all is!' he exclaimed wryly, yet at the same time acknowledging, 'It is plain I must go no further on this road: if you and he cannot understand me who will?' (LB 272–3).

That Nature is a Heraclitean Fire and of The comfort of the Resurrection

Heraclitus was a fifth century BC Greek philosopher who believed that all things were in a state of flux and were ultimately resolvable into the element of fire. The poem begins with a vividly realised sense of Heraclitean process. First of all, clouds are imaged in a variety of striking metaphors as they either progress down their aerial 'thoroughfare' like so many ebullient 'gangs', or in more orderly fashion in 'marches'. Light, filtering through the moving branches of elms creates shafts and networks of shadow ('Shivelights and shadowtackle') down 'roughcast' and whitewashed walls, constantly creating and recreating new formations of pattern ('lace, lance, and pair'). The wind's erosion effaces all trace of unevenness on the earth caused by the previous day's ('yestertempest's') storm, gradually drying out ('parches') the mud at the edges of pools and wheel ruts, turning it to a dry 'crust' and then to dust. The wind dries and stiffens myriads ('squadroned') of marks made in the earth by the feet of working men ('treadmire toil' cf. 'trod'; 'God's Grandeur'), and all this movement fuels a million-fold 'nature's bonfire', an image used by Heraclitus himself in one of his extant fragments.

---

1   In Manchester City Art Gallery: it can be seen at http://www.ibiblio.org/wm/paint/auth/brown

Tragically, however, not even man, 'life's pride and cared-for crown' ('The Sea and the Skylark'), is exempt from this flux, being in fact little more than a 'spark' in the general conflagration. His own physical 'firedint' (or 'forged feature'; 'Henry Purcell') is soon obliterated along with the mark his mind makes on the universal reason. 'Both' body and mind are drowned in what Hopkins describes in a Wordsworthian polysyllable as an 'unfathomable [...]dark'. The self of an individual as separate, and shining as a star in the sky, suffers instant eclipse at death ('death blots black out'). Time 'beats level' the distinctive mark of each and ensures that even remembrance is lost in 'vastness'. The ideas are similar to those in 'The Lantern out of Doors' and are perhaps anticipated many years previously in a fragment from an abandoned play of Hopkins, 'I am like a slip of comet' (1864) where the comet, having made its journey, 'then goes out into the cavernous dark' like the poet at the end of his life, 'So I go out' (ll.16–17).[1] Such apparent hopelessness makes him cry out in grief, 'O pity and indignation!'

In *Studies in the History of the Renaissance* (1873) Hopkins's one time Oxford tutor, Walter Pater, stressed the significance of exploiting the aesthetic 'moment' in a world he, too, describes in Heraclitean terms:

> While all melts under our feet, we may well grasp at any exquisite passion or any contribution to knowledge that seems by a lifted horizon to set the spirit free for a moment [...] Not to discriminate every moment some passionate attitude in those about us [...] is on this short day of frost and sun, to sleep before evening.

Like Hopkins, Pater is only too aware of what he calls 'the splendour of our experience and of its awful brevity'. His concept of success is famously for man 'To burn always with [a] hard, gemlike flame, to maintain this ecstasy'. For Hopkins, however, in such shifting circumstances, the aesthetic moment is inadequate, in fact meaningless, without 'the comfort of the resurrection'. And the 'volta', or turning-point, in this extended sonnet puts a sudden end to despair, 'Enough!' The promise of the risen Christ wakens the dispirited heart like a clarion call. 'Joyless days, dejection', a phrase resonant with Romantic *weltschmerz*, are cancelled as a light of rescue shines across the 'foundering deck' of a life 'gasping' for air and about to be 'Drowned' (l.13) in 'an enormous dark' (l.12).

The poem approaches its conclusion by adapting the words of St Paul:

---

1   Phillips, p.40

We shall not all sleep, but we shall all be changed, in a moment, in the twinkling of an eye, at the last trump: for the trumpet shall sound, and the dead shall be raised incorruptible, and we shall be changed. For this corruptible must put on incorruption, and this mortal *must* put on immortality (Cor.1,Ch.15, v. 51–3).

All, therefore, that is 'residuary', a legal term meaning what is left of an estate, in this case man's mortal flesh, falls to its inheritor, the 'worm'. Only 'dust' (l.7) and 'ash' (l.20) are left ('for dust thou art, and unto dust shalt thou return' Genesis, Ch.3, v.19). However, 'in a moment', as St Paul promises ('In a flash [...] all at once') – not to be confused with the aesthetic 'moment' of Walter Pater – we are immortalised, through Christ having once been himself what now we are, mortal. The last line of the poem transmutes, without change of emphasis, the humble self ('jack') as a joke, a piece of broken pottery, a fool ('patch') and splinter of wood into 'immortal diamond'. The triumph of Christ's resurrection is compounded in the repetition, 'Is immortal diamond'. Hopkins's contempt for the 'mortal' part of man here, however, is at variance with his more strict adherence to the Catholic dogma of the resurrection of the body, 'Man's spirit will be flesh-bound, when found at best' (see 'The Caged Skylark').

Justus quidem tu es, Domine

In the first quatrain Hopkins renders a verse from Jeremiah (Jer., xii, 1) into the form of a 'complaint' recalling Donne's logical interrogation of God in 'If poisonous mineralls'.[1] It is as though in their idle moments drunks and the slaves of lust are rewarded more by this God who, in his attempts to defeat his devoted servant, seems vindictively perverse. The slightly querulous register here is tempered, however, by the reverence of Hopkins's form of address, 'Sir' – a reverence that reminds us of George Herbert - and his underlying tone of conviction in God's goodness which results in the gentle plea of the final line. In the sestet Hopkins echoes the language of Herbert's 'Affliction (1)':

> I read and sigh, and wish I were a tree –
>   For sure, then, I should grow
> To fruit or shade; at least, some bird would trust
> Her household to me, and I should be just.

---

1   John Donne,'Holy Sonnet, IX'

This poignant sonnet, written a few months before his death, reflects the sentiments to be found in a letter to Bridges a year or more before its composition: 'All impulse fails me: I can give myself no sufficient reason for going on. Nothing comes: I am a eunuch – but it is for the kingdom of heaven's sake' (LB 270) (cf. Matthew, Ch.19, v. 12). As in Coleridge's 'Dejection: an Ode', however, the announcement of a deficiency results in a poem ironically testifying to its author's continuing creative abilities (cf. 'To R.B.).

To R.B.

Hopkins's poem to Robert Bridges, is his final 'explanation' for a perceived inability to create, and in some ways stands as an 'apology' for what he considered to be his many wider failures. The first quatrain associates inspiration with the sexual act. The absent father, or begetter, of the poem is the muse, whose fiery impregnation bears similarities to Shelley's concept of 'the mind in creation [...] as a fading coal', and of how 'when composition begins, inspiration is already on the decline'[1] The poet/mother of the second quatrain, and now 'The widow of an insight lost', has responsibility for carrying, rearing and grooming the child/poem, product of the original inspiration. The process is skilful ('hand at work now never wrong') and the fine-tuning lengthy, where the nine months of gestation may result in as many as the 'nine years' Horace had suggested in *The Art of Poetry* as an appropriate period for poetic revision. As in 'Justus quidem', Hopkins describes a period of creative dearth. His 'winter world' shares with that sonnet the sense of Coleridgean dejection as well as Coleridge's sentiments in his 'Work Without Hope':

> [...] All nature seems at work. Slugs leave their lair –
> The bees are stirring – birds are on the wing –
> And Winter slumbering in the open air,
> Wears on his smiling face a dream of Spring!
> And I the while, the sole unbusy thing,
> Nor honey make, nor pair, nor build, nor sing.

Beneath the overt statements on writing lie, perhaps, more poignant feelings of solitude, the celibate's lack of a shared 'delight', 'rapture', 'bliss' and in whose 'lagging lines' is the sorrowful sense of having fallen behind in the race, the 'lonely began' of 'To seem the stranger'. Once more, however, Hopkins's achievement in 'To R. B.'

---

1   *A Defence of Poetry*, 1820

belies its stated theme. It is even more appropriate that this, his final poem, should be addressed to Robert Bridges who, after a much more lengthy period than that of which the poem speaks, would finally ensure his friend's enduring fame.

Part 4. Reception

At the time of his death Hopkins's poetry was known only to a very few number of people. The manuscript poems were carefully preserved by Robert Bridges and, among his other friends, only Richard Watson Dixon and Coventry Patmore shared Bridges's knowledge of his talents as a poet. Dixon, who had been a teacher at Highgate School during part of Hopkins's time there, was an Anglican minister when, many years later, he received a letter from Hopkins (LD 1–3) declaring admiration for his practically unknown poetry, and it was from this time that they became regular correspondents. In turn an unequivocal admirer of Hopkins's work, Dixon tried unsuccessfully to get him to agree to publication hoping that the Jesuit order would not stand in the way. He wrote: 'Surely one vocation cannot destroy another: and such a Society as yours will not remain ignorant that you have such gifts as have seldom been given by God to man' (LD 90).

Hopkins met Coventry Patmore, a co-religionist and whose poetry he had admired from undergraduate days, when Patmore was invited as special guest to a speech day at Stonyhurst in 1883. They, too, became friends and correspondents. Although Patmore assured Hopkins that he would always regard 'my having made your acquaintance as an important event of my life' (FL 363), his views on his poetry were nonetheless politely critical. He saw Hopkins's theories and what he called his 'obscuring novelty of mode' acting as 'self-imposed shackles' on thoughts which would otherwise '"*voluntary* move harmonious numbers"'. To the 'arduous' character of his poetry Hopkins had added, in Patmore's view:

> [...] the difficulty of following *several* entirely novel and simultaneous experiments in versification and construction, together with an altogether unprecedented system of alliteration and compound words; - any one of which novelties would be startling and productive of distraction from the poetic matter to be expressed' (FL 352–3).

Patmore believed, therefore, that Hopkins's poetry would be 'of a kind to appeal only to the few' (ibid.), describing it to Bridges as being like 'veins of pure gold imbedded in masses of unpracticable quartz' (FL 353n.).

During the years between his death and the 1918 publication, a few of Hopkins's poems appeared in a handful of anthologies, including an important war-time collection, *The Spirit of Man*, edited by Bridges himself in 1917. By the time the *Poems* appeared in the following year, therefore, interest had already been awakened, although it was not until the Charles Williams edition, *Poetry of Hopkins* in 1930, that the work began to attract a significant volume of critical attention.

Hopkins told Baillie in 1885 that he made 'no attempt to publish' (FL 257), but admitted in the following year that 'fame, the being known, though in itself one of the most dangerous things to man, is nevertheless the true and appointed air, element, and setting of genius and its works' (LB 231). Some critical judgements on the tensions in Hopkins's poetry, such as those between his aesthetic and ascetic inclinations, have tended to see them as sexual in origin. The critic, Bernard Bergonzi, however, regards these kinds of conflict as the product of a Hopkins divided between, on the one hand, his Jesuitical desire for self-effacement and a yearning for literary acknowledgement on the other.[1] Certainly, Hopkins appears relatively sanguine about his work becoming more widely known when he writes to Bridges in 1878: 'What you have got of mine you may do as you like with about shewing to friends' (LB 54), and to Dixon in 1881 he writes of how 'in the midst of outward occupations not only the mind is drawn away from God [...] but [...] worldly interests freshen, and worldly ambitions revive' (LD 75–6). Two weeks later, however, he writes to him:

> The question [...] for me is not whether I am willing [...] to make a sacrifice of hopes of fame [...] but whether I am not to undergo a severe judgment from God for the lothness I have shewn in making it [...] for the waste of time the very compositions you admire may have caused and their preoccupation of the mind which belonged to more sacred or more binding duties, for the disquiet and the thoughts of vainglory they have given rise to (LD 88).

As he told Dixon very early in their correspondence: 'the only just literary critic is Christ, who prizes, is proud of, and admires, more than any man [...] the gifts of his own making' (LD 8), and later makes of Christ his great example on the question of failure and success, in phrasing which anticipates that of his own sonnets of desolation: '[...] his career was cut short and, whereas he would have wished to succeed by success [...] nevertheless he was doomed to succeed by failure; his plans were baffled, his hopes dashed, and his work was done by being broken off undone' (LD 137–8).

The importance of Hopkins's vocation cannot be overstressed in any critical assessment of his work. His conversion to Catholicism, like that of any devout Victorian

---

1   Bernard Bergonzi, *Gerard Manley Hopkins* (London: Macmillan, 1992), p.150

brought up within the Anglican tradition, was the major event of his life, so that his decision to become a priest became, for someone of his convictions, the only imaginable way forward. He wrote to Baillie in the critical period before deciding to be a Catholic:

> You will no doubt understand what I mean by saying that the *sordidness* of things wh. one is compelled perpetually to feel, is perhaps [...] the most unmixedly painful thing one knows of: and this is (objectively) intensified and (subjectively) destroyed by Catholicism. If people cd. all know this [...] no other inducement wd. to very many minds be needed to lead them to Catholicism and no opposite inducement cd. dissuade them fr. it (FL 226–7).

For most people the degree of Hopkins's discipline and assiduousness would seem to be entirely out of reach, yet to Dixon he could write in 1881, 'I have never wavered in my vocation, but I have not lived up to it' (LD 88). Such high idealism and unshakeable faith is perhaps always challenging and it may be that, at bottom, it was blank incomprehension that affected the way Bridges wrote in the *Preface* to his edition. Although he is objectively critical of the poetry's 'Oddity and Obscurity', some of his language about what he calls 'questions of taste', 'affectation' and 'perversion of human feeling' might have been shaped by Hopkins's efforts at times, as he sees it, 'to force emotion into theological or sectarian channels'. That Bridges did not share his religious beliefs was a matter of great concern to Hopkins ('You understand of course that I desire to see you a Catholic or [...] at least a believer in the true God', LB 60) who, on one occasion, chastised his visiting friend for his unresponsiveness to a Catholic 'Corpus Christi' procession:

> It is long since such things had any significance for you. But what is strange and unpleasant is that you sometimes speak as if they had in reality none for me and you were only awaiting with a certain disgust till I too should be disgusted with myself enough to throw off the mask (LB 148).

It is possible to argue persuasively, like Joan Bennett, that even though a 'precedent knowledge of the Catholic doctrine [of the resurrection of the body] is necessary' for a poem such as 'The Caged Skylark' to be understood, a reader is not obliged to share the poet's beliefs to appreciate his poetry.[1] Nevertheless, ever since Bridges first raised it as an issue, the profoundly religious and Catholic nature of Hopkins's work has continued to influence critical assessment. In 1932, for example, Herbert Read

---

1   Joan Bennett, *Four Metaphysical Poets*, Cambridge, 1934 cited from Gerald Roberts, *op.cit.* p.290

believed that Hopkins 'might have ranged widely in intellectual curiosity had he not preferred to submit to authority' and could not help regretting 'the curtailment [his work] suffered in range and quantity'.[1] Cecil Day Lewis spoke in 1937 of the 'blight the trivial and ludicrous minutiae of Catholic doctrine had cast upon the poet's intelligence'.[2] Seamus Heaney, in a British Academy lecture of 1974, talks of Hopkins's sonnet, 'Spring' as 'structurally a broken arch, with an octave of description aspiring towards a conjunction with a sestet of doctrine',[3] and Hopkins's most recent biographer, Norman White, writes that it appears to him that in 'The Starlight Night' the poet's 'urgent responses' in the octave have been 'blotted out and replaced' by 'conventional response' in the sestet.[4]

In 1935 Father Joseph Keating, editor of *The Month*, raised the issue of unsympathetic critical judgements (including those of Claude Colleer Abbott, editor of the correspondence with Bridges and Dixon). 'The fact is', he writes, these are the judgements of critics who:

> do not share the faith of their subject, they regard it as unsound and erroneous, they are more or less hostile to it, they resent its interference with his poetic work, and so, not understanding or appreciating it, they cannot fully understand or appreciate him.[5]

In the introduction to his edition of the Hopkins-Bridges correspondence, Abbott writes of the 'insuperable barrier' Hopkins's priesthood presented to Bridges and of how Bridges 'had, and rightly, a profound distrust of the Society of Jesus' (LB xlv). Quoting this, and italicising the word 'rightly', Father Keating remarks that Abbott, like Bridges, labours under a handicap in his approach to Hopkins. He assumes

> that a vocation to the religious state is on the same level and of the same character as a "vocation" to be a poet, that God, by conferring exceptional talents, thereby virtually imposes an obligation to use them. That is not the Catholic view, as Hopkins pointed out at length (*op.cit.*).

The impasse over the issue of Hopkins as priest-poet, or poet compromised by priest-

---

1   Herbert Read, *Form in Modern Poetry*, London, 1932, cited from Gerald Roberts, *op.cit.* p.244
2   C. Day Lewis, 'Gerard Manley Hopkins, Poet and Jesuit', *Left Review*, April, 1937, cited from Gerald Roberts, *op.cit.* p.371
3   Seamus Heaney, British Academy Lecture, 1974, cited from Norman H. Mackenzie, *A Reader s Guide to Gerard Manley Hopkins* (London: Thames & Hudson, 1981) p.70
4   Norman White, *Hopkins: A Literary Biography* (Oxford: Clarendon Press, 1992), p.268
5   Fr Joseph Keating, review, *The Month*, February, 1935, cited from Gerald Roberts, *op.cit.* p.302

hood, is unlikely to be resolved by argument. It is akin to another critical debate arising over whether his poetry's literary place belongs properly to the nineteenth or twentieth centuries. Whether as poetry it is Victorian in sentiment, first and foremost, or essentially Modernist in style and technique.

Alison Sulloway considers Hopkins to be Victorian in 'Temper', but in the broadest sense that, in any estimation of Victorianism, moods reflecting 'unqualified optimism' and 'the blackest distress' can be equally representative of the period. It is in what she calls 'this shifting spirit, now exuberant, now tentatively hopeful, or at least reconciliatory, now gloomy, if not actually apocalyptic' that Hopkins can be said to be truly Victorian.[1] For F.R.Leavis in 1932, Hopkins was a figure who, because of his publication history, inevitably spanned both centuries and was 'likely to prove, for our time and the future, the only influential poet of the Victorian age'; and of that age, Leavis adds, 'he seems to me the greatest.'[2] Leavis remarks that Hopkins's genius is proved by the 'strength and subtlety of his imagery' and that Victorian poetry, lacking such virtues, would have been reconstituted by an acceptance of his work. However, because Hopkins was unpublished in 1889 he is 'now felt to be a contemporary', he writes, and his technique 'so much concerned with inner division, friction, and psychological complexities in general has a special bearing on the problems of contemporary poetry.' Bernard Bergonzi also believes that it is 'conceivable' that, had Hopkins been published earlier, he might have changed the course of English poetry in the latter part of the nineteenth century. But it is more likely, he writes, 'that he would have been regarded as an oddity, with few readers and no noticeable influence.'[3] He believes, therefore, that Bridges's extreme caution in delaying publication for almost thirty years was judicious in its timing.

For Robert Graves and Laura Riding, writing in 1927, Hopkins was a poet who had made of poetry 'a higher sort of psychology.'[4] They describe him as a modernist, 'in virtue of his extraordinary strictures in the use of words and the unconventional notation he used in setting them down so that *they had to be understood as he meant them to be, or understood not at all.*' Graves and Riding are highly critical of Bridges where he talks in his *Preface* of Hopkins's 'blemishes' being 'of such quality and magnitude as to deny him even a hearing from those who love a continuous

---

1   A. Sulloway, *Gerard Manley Hopkins and the Victorian Temper* (London: Routledge & Kegan Paul, 1972), p 1.

2   F. R. Leavis, *op.cit.*, p.193

3   Bernard Bergonzi, *Gerard Manley Hopkins, op.cit.* p.86

4   Laura Riding and Robert Graves, A *Survey of Modernist Poetry*, 1927, cited from Gerald Roberts, *op.cit.* p.146, p.148

literary decorum'. By breeching this so-called literary decorum, they write, Bridges was objecting not primarily to Hopkins's 'faults of taste or style but to 'a daring that makes the past socially rather than artistically objectionable.' To argue in this way about Hopkins's treatment by Bridges 'and other upholders of "literary decorum"' is reminiscent of critics who have seen contemporary attacks on Keats's poetry as equally socially motivated.

The extraordinarily innovative language of Hopkins's work made it an obvious subject for the Practical Criticism and American New Criticism schools of the earlier twentieth century, and it continues to lend itself rewardingly to the kind of close reading with which these critical approaches were associated. After Bridges, Hopkins's next editor, Charles Williams, in his Introduction to the Second Edition of 1930, believed Milton to be 'the poet to whom we should most relate Gerard Hopkins', while F. R. Leavis thought that in his 'imagery, and his way of using the body and movement of the language' Hopkins was closer to Shakespeare. The critic Donald Davie also acknowledged that his use of language was Shakespearean in its audacity, but that whereas Shakespeare was disrespectful of a language 'still in the meltingpot, fluid, experimental and expanding rapidly', Hopkins treated contemporary English 'as if it were still unstable and immature.'[1] C. Day Lewis, in 1947, believed that Hopkins in this sense was an 'unconscious revolutionary;' that where Wordsworth might have deliberately rebelled against the conventions and tutored diction of his time, Hopkins's innovations 'spring from a kind of innocent experimenting with words, as a child of genius might invent a new style of architecture while playing with bricks!'[2]

James Milroy, who focuses particularly on the language of Hopkins, stresses his use of words in the native English tradition as such words 'contract much more complex, subtle and far-reaching networks of relationship within the language than do Classical borrowings.'[3] Bernard Bergonzi sees this use of a native idiom as an expression of Hopkins's 'profound English patriotism and sense of identity' – an aspect of the poet which aligns him much more closely with his Victorian contemporaries than with their successors.[4]

Especially prominent among the many critics who have subjected the poetry to close linguistic analysis is William Empson who, in his discussion of the notorious crux, 'Buckle', in 'The Windhover', accentuated the modernist psychological dimen-

---

1   D. Davie, *Purity of Diction in English Verse* (London: Routledge & Kegan Paul, 1967), p.175
2   C. Day Lewis, *op.cit.*, p.8
3   J. Milroy, *The Language of Gerard Manley Hopkins* (London: Andre Deutsch, 1977), p.156
4   Bergonzi, *Gerard Manley Hopkins, op.cit.* p.169

sion in Hopkins which had been commented on by others. Empson identified in the first three lines of the sonnet's sestet 'a clear case of the Freudian use of opposites, where two things thought of as incompatible, but desired intensely by different systems of judgement, are spoken of simultaneously by words applying to both.' In our very process of reading the lines, therefore, Empson maintains that 'two systems of judgement are forced into open conflict before the reader.'[1] Bergonzi adds that Hopkins would have known well enough what he wanted to say and was very clear in a letter to Bridges (LB 169) about his intended meaning of the potentially ambiguous word 'foil' in 'God's Grandeur'. In 'The Windhover', however, through not always realising 'the confusion he was causing by the insufficiently considered use of a simple noun with several meanings and no clue from the context,' Hopkins has left, writes Bergonzi, a 'disabling ambiguity' which, depending on how the word 'buckle' is construed, can alter the whole meaning of the poem.[2]

The emphasis which Hopkins placed on the performance and speech element of his poems has led to criticism which looks at his attempt to communicate through the 'printed voice.' Eric Griffiths, in a monograph of that title, examines Hopkins's poetry to demonstrate how meaning in a poem can often depend upon the declamation or pronouncement of particular lines or even, in some cases, how a poem can 'mean' through what it equally does *not* say.[3] In the sonnet, 'To seem the stranger', for example, 'Father and mother dear, /Brothers and sisters are in Christ not near', reverses the form of address, 'dear Father and Mother', compounding Hopkins's estrangement with its sense of a letter unsent. [The sonnet, 'I wake and feel' does indeed use the image of 'cries' as 'dead letters sent/To dearest him that lives alas! away']. The comfort of the wishful phrase 'are in Christ' is cancelled by 'not near', which, as *spoken*, conveys a desolation which would be absent from the conventional phrasing, 'Brothers and sisters are not near in Christ'. Again, Hopkins's use of the oblique in 'he my peace/my parting' is an example of what, Griffiths says, 'cannot be spoken and yet it is that in the line which most needs to be said.'

Hopkins's celibacy, the evidence throughout his writings of his interest in male physique and beauty, his unusually expressive love for Christ ('the only person I am in love with' LB 66), and the struggle he obviously experienced between religious discipline and the sensuality of his responses, has made a troubled sexuality the basis

---

1   W. Empson, *Seven Types of Ambiguity* (London: Chatto & Windus, 1930, revised 1953), pp.225–6
2   Bergonzi, *Gerard Manley Hopkins*, op.cit. p.182
3   E. Griffiths, *The Printed Voice of Victorian Poetry* (Oxford: Clarendon Press, 1989), p.299

of some important modern criticism. It has been pointed out that there are very few female figures in the poetry and those which do occur tend to be virgins or virgin-martyrs (for example, Margaret Clitheroe, St Winefred, the nun of 'The Wreck of the Deutschland'). There is a case for saying, of course, that Hopkins's vocation placed inevitable restrictions on his experience, but that women in his poetry are often the victims of violence has provoked comment. A seminal essay by Thaïs E. Morgan on *The Wreck*, for example, takes what it sees as the highly sexualised language of the poem as the starting point for an argument that Hopkins displaces his homoerotic love for Christ on to the nun, acts as voyeur and then destroys her. Having inscribed 'an emergent homosexual identity into his text,' he finally 'asserts his preference for a less sensual, less threatening, more "manly," and more conventional "measure" of showing his devotion to Christ.'[1] Isabel Armstrong, on similar lines, finds indications in the syntax of *The Wreck* of Hopkins's dual sexual identity insofar as his 'male' nun, who 'rears' herself to Christ, takes on his qualities while he, in being asked to 'come quickly', takes on hers.[2] Michael Lynch, writing on 'Pied Beauty', also finds in the phraseology of the poem a coded expression of Hopkins's sexual nature.[3]

Hopkins appears to have regarded his proclivities as intrinsically sinful, keeping notes as an undergraduate about sins to be confessed, all of which gets discussed in Paddy Kitchen's biography of 1978.[4] It was a sense of this need to keep virtue intact which probably made Hopkins assert so strongly his resistance to any close iden-tification of his own poetry with the homoerotic verse of the American poet, Walt Whitman. The following may have been in response to remarks of Bridges, though it must remain speculative since all Bridges's side of his correspondence with Hopkins has been lost:

> [...] I may as well say what I should not otherwise have said, that I always knew in my heart Walt Whitman's mind to be more like my own than any other man's living. As he is a very great scoundrel this is not a pleasant con-fession. And this also makes me the more desirous to read him and the more determined that I will not (LB 155).

In an essay written for the Master of Balliol in 1864 entitled 'On the Signs of Health

---

1   T. E. Morgan, 'Violence, Creativity, and the Feminine: Poetics and Gender Politics in Swinburne and Hopkins', in A. H. Harrison and B. Taylor eds. *Gender and Discourse in Victorian Literature and Art* (DeKalb, Ill.: North Illinois University Press, 1992), pp.94–5

2   I. Armstrong, *Victorian Poetry: Poetry, Poetics and Politics* (London: Routledge, 1993), p.433

3   M. Lynch, 'Recovering Hopkins, Recovering Ourselves' (*Hopkins Quarterly*, 1979, 6).

4   P. Kitchen, *Gerard Manley Hopkins* (London, Hamish Hamilton, 1978), Ch.4.

and decay in the Arts', Hopkins ascribed signs of 'decay and weakness' to the 'poetry of the United States' (J 79), and there is evidence from his letter to Bridges (ibid.) that he had some familiarity by this time with Whitman's *Leaves of Grass* (1855).

Issues of gender in Hopkins are discussed in relation to his concept of poetic creativity by the feminist critics Sandra Gilbert and Susan Gubar. They argue that in his identification with the emasculated 'eunuch' ('Justus quidem') or in his description of himself as 'the widow of an insight lost' ('To R. B.'), Hopkins recognises the submissive role of woman in a world of predominantly generative male literary power. In 'To R.B.', for example, this is expressed phallically in the all-powerful 'live and lancing [...] blowpipe flame'.[1] Alison Sulloway identifies in 'God's Grandeur' a positive female counter-principle in the 'dearest freshness deep down things' working against two male symbols, one of grandeur and the other of industrial spoliation, a male 'rape of the countryside.'[2] Helen Vendler, on the other hand, sees the writing of *The Wreck* as a form of male enfranchisement, an affirmation of Hopkins's own adulthood in that he may have thought of his poet-father (a marine insurance adjuster) as the rightful owner ('the frown of his face') of both poetry *and* shipwrecks and of himself as a usurper of these rights. Vendler detects in Hopkins's poem an indication of 'one of those individual talents (to use Eliot's words) that force the whole poetic tradition in English into its rare historic realignments.'[3]

Of the great twentieth century Hopkins scholars, W. H. Gardner saw him as situated firmly within that English tradition, as a poet who, in the 'Terrible Sonnets', for example, equalled at times Shakespeare's own tragic voice.[4] F. R. Leavis, as mentioned earlier, regarded Hopkins not only as the greatest voice among Victorian poets, but saw in his poetry also a psychology and technique which, taking him well beyond his own times, made him influential as modernist and formalist.

There have also been dissenting voices. The American poet and critic, Yvor Winters, found a disconcerting note in Hopkins which was, he believed, traceable to Romanticism with its 'tendency to suppress the rational in poetry.'[5] In a discussion of

---

1   S. M. Gilbert and S. Gubar, *The Madwoman in the Attic: The Woman Writer and the Nineteenth-Century Literary Imagination* (New Haven and London: Yale University Press, second printing, 1980), p.10

2   A. Sulloway, 'Gerard Manley Hopkins and 'Women and Men' as Partners in the Mystery of Redemption', *Texas Studies in Literature and Language*, 31 (1), p.45

3   H. Vendler, 'The Wreck of the Deutschland' in A. Mortimer ed. *The Authentic Cadence: Centennial Essays on Gerard Manley Hopkins* (Fribourg: University Press of Fribourg, 1992), p.51

4   W. H. Gardner, *Gerard Manley Hopkins: A Study of Poetic Idiosyncrasy in Relation to Poetic Tradition* (London: Secker & Warburg, 1944, 1949), 2 Vols, Vol.1, pp.174-9

5   Y. Winters, *The Function of Criticism: Problems and Exercises* (London: Routledge & Kegan Paul,

'The Windhover' he queries Hopkins's responses, describing his poetry as 'a chaos of details afloat in vague emotion.'[1]

The poetry of Hopkins has a particularly topical relevance at the turn of the century in the field of ecological studies. His heightened awareness of the precariousness of the natural environment in his own nineteenth century is evident in poems such as 'Duns Scotus's Oxford', 'Inversnaid' and 'Binsey Poplars'. To Bridges in 1855 he writes, 'they are there yet', when describing a recent family visit to 'a lovely landscape' in Sussex (LB 220); and again, a few weeks later, of the 'quarrying away' of mountains in Wales: 'nowhere I suppose in Europe is such a subjection of nature to man to be witnessed' (LB 226). Jonathan Bate traces to Hopkins's 'Inversnaid' a direct line from Wordsworth's 'The Ruined Cottage' and the poetry of John Clare in their proposal that 'the survival of humanity comes with nature's mastery over the edifices of civilisation.'[2] Clare's poem, 'I am! Yet what I am who cares or knows?' is copied by Hopkins into his diary for 1865, and he shared with both Wordsworth and Clare a sense that poetry does not belong to the study but is inspired by a direct experience of the natural world. For all three poets composition took the form of a peripatetic activity. To Dixon in July 1888 Hopkins writes: 'there was one windy bright day between floods last week [...] I put work aside and went out for the day, and conceived a sonnet' (LD 157). Another sonnet, 'St Alphonsus Rodriguez', he tells Bridges, 'was made out of doors...with my mind's eye on the first presentment of the thought' (LB 297).

There is much evidence from H. D. Rawnsley who, with Octavia Hill and Robert Hunter, founded The National Trust,[3] that the 'Peasantry of Westmoreland' was intrigued by Wordsworth's habit of composing on the hoof, and that his custom of talking to himself was responsible for something of his reputation for being slightly unhinged:

> But he talked a deal to hissen. I often seead his lips a gaäin, and he'd a deal o' mumblin' to hissel, and 'ud stop short and be lookin' down upo' the ground, as if he was in a thinking waäy.[4]

1962), p.104

1   *ibid.* p.145

2   Jonathan Bate, *Romantic Ecology: Wordsworth and the Environmental Tradition* (London and New York, Routledge, 1991), p. 34

3   The National Trust is a foundation which was set up in 1895 to act as a guardian for the nation in the acquisition and protection of threatened coastline, countryside and buildings.

4   H. D. Rawnsley, *Reminiscences of Wordsworth among the Peasantry of Westmoreland.*

Hopkins said that he had no knowledge of Rawnsley (LB 139), but a reminiscence by an old lay brother of the poet at Stonyhurst has an interesting resemblance to Rawnsley's anecdotes of Wordsworth:

> One of Hopkins's special delights, said the brother, was the path from the seminary to the College. After a shower, he would run and crouch down to gaze at the crushed quartz glittering as the sun came out again. "Ay, a strange young man", said the old brother, "crouching down that gate to stare at some wet sand. A fair natural 'e seemed to us, that Mr.'opkins" (J 408, editor's note).

The extraordinary and attractive poetry of Gerard Manley Hopkins, with its passionate involvement in the beauties of creation has had admirers since first publication. In some ways Hopkins's profound spirituality, his single-minded commitment and the pressure of intelligence behind his convictions, continues to make him a mysterious figure, and this in spite of the accessibility of his letters, notebooks and journals as well as the academic research which all the time discovers new materials and often surprising and topically relevant details about him. Hopkins was an intellectual with a rare poetic gift. But in the end he used that gift, setting aside personal fame and ambition, for the purpose that, as a Jesuit, he believed it should be exclusively used, God only 'to aggrandise, God to glorify'.[1]

---

1   'The Candle Indoors'

5. Bibliography

5.1 List of Abbreviations Used in the Text

LB. Claude Colleer Abbott ed., *The Letters of Gerard Manley Hopkins to Robert Bridges* (London: Oxford University Press, 1935).

LD. Claude Colleer Abbott ed., *The Correspondence of Gerard Manley Hopkins and Richard Watson Dixon* (London: Oxford University Press, 1935)

FL. Claude Colleer Abbott ed., *Further Letters of Gerard Manley Hopkins, Including his Correspondence With Gerard Manley Hopkins* 2nd rev. edn reprinted 1970 (London: Oxford University Press, 1956).

J. Humphry House ed., completed by Graham Storey, *The Journals and Papers of Gerard Manley Hopkins* (London: Oxford University Press, 1959).

SD Christopher Devlin ed., *The Sermons and Devotional Writings of Gerard Manley Hopkins* (London: Oxford University Press, 1959).

Phillips Catherine Phillips ed., *Gerard Manley Hopkins* (Oxford: Oxford University Press, 1986; repr. Oxford World's Classics, 2002).

5.2 Recommended Reading

Biography

Bernard Bergonzi, *Gerard Manley Hopkins* (London: Macmillan, 1977).
Robert Bernard Martin, *Gerard Manley Hopkins: A Very Private Life* (London: HarperCollins, 1991).
Norman White, *Hopkins: A Literary Biography* (Oxford: Clarendon Press, 1992).

Criticism

John Pick, *Gerard Manley Hopkins: Priest and Poet* (London: Oxford University Press, 1942, 2nd edn 1966).

Donald McChesney, *A Hopkins Commentary* (London: University of London Press, 1968).

Alfred Thomas, *Hopkins the Jesuit: The Years of Training* (London: Oxford University Press, 1969).

R. K. R. Thornton, *Gerard Manley Hopkins: The Poems* (London: Edward Arnold, 1973).

R. K. R. Thornton, *All My Eyes See: The Visual World of Gerard Manley Hopkins* (Sunderland, Ceolfrith Press, 1975).

Norman H. Mackenzie, *A Reader's Guide to Gerard Manley Hopkins* (London: Thames & Hudson, 1981)

Gerald Roberts, ed. *Gerard Manley Hopkins: The Critical Heritage* (London: Routledge & Kegan Paul, 1987).

Graham Storey, *A Preface to Hopkins* (London: Longman 1981, 2nd edn 1992).

Daniel Brown, *Hopkins's Idealism: Philosophy, Physics, Poetry* (Oxford: Clarendon Press, 1997).

Alice Jenkins, *The Poems of Gerard Manley Hopkins: A Sourcebook* (London: Routledge, 2006).

Websites

http://www.literaryhistory.com/19thC/HOPKINS.htm (A very useful Web guide to Hopkins).

http://www.dundee.ac.uk/english/wics/gmh/framconc.htm (An online concordance which allows a search of the poems for a given word; it includes and is based on the Bridges (1918) edition.

www.gerardmanleyhopkins.org/festival (Information on the annual Gerard Manley Hopkins International Summer School)

Appendices

Robert Bridges, Author's Preface, Poems, 1918

Our generation already is overpast,
And thy lov'd legacy, Gerard, hath lain
Coy in my home; as once thy heart was fain
Of shelter, when God's terror held thee fast
In life's wild wood at Beauty and Sorrow aghast;
Thy sainted sense trammel'd in ghostly pain,
Thy rare ill-broker'd talent in disdain:
Yet love of Christ will win man's love at last.

Hell wars without; but, dear, the while my hands
Gather'd thy book, I heard, this wintry day,
Thy spirit thank me, in his young delight
Stepping again upon the yellow sands.
Go forth: amidst our chaffinch flock display
Thy plumage of far wonder and heavenward flight!

Hopkins favoured the sonnet

Many poets have found the sonnet form very useful. Precisely because it has been used so often, it carries a lot of baggage, and a writer is always making space for himself against the inheritance of the past, the memory of how a form has been used before. The association of the sonnet with love poetry, for example, is clearly of importance to George Herbert and to Hopkins.

Formally, the sonnet, in its division in its Petrarchan form into octave and sestet, offers in a small compass the chance to deploy a serious argument. The sestet often replies to or counters the octave. The English form, with three quatrains and a couplet, also offers space to develop an idea and offer a counter to it. Renaissance sonnets, as Hopkins well knew, are often experimental metrically and formally and some have more, some less than the fourteen lines we have come to recognise as diagnostic. (Shakespeare 126 has only 12 lines, for example.)

The Sea and the Skylark

Hopkins wrote to Bridges explaining in detail his intentions in describing the flight of the skylark. It gives some impression of the kind of detailed observation which went into the construction of his lines.

> The skein and coil are the lark's song, which from his height gives the impression (not to me only) of something falling to the earth and not vertically quite but tricklingly or wavingly, something as a skein of silk ribbed by having been tightly wound on a narrow card or a notched holder or as fishingtackle or twine unwinding from a reel or winch: the laps or folds are the notes or short measures and bars of them. The same is called a score in the musical sense of score and this score is 'writ upon a liquid sky trembling to welcome it', only not horizontally. The lark in wild glee races the reel round, paying or dealing out and down the turns of the skein or coil right to the earth floor, the ground, where it lies in a heap, as it were, or rather is all wound off on to another winch, reel, bobbin, or spool in Fancy's eye by the moment the bird touches earth and so is ready for a fresh unwinding at the next flight (LB 164).

Ford Madox Brown: For the Picture called 'Work'

WORK! Which beads the brow, and tans the flesh
Of lusty manhood, casting out its devils!
By whose weird art transmuting poor men's evils,
Their bed seems down, their one dish ever fresh.
Ah me! For lack of it what ills in leash
Hold us. 'Tis want the pale mechanic levels
To workhouse depths, while Master Spendthrift revels.
For want of work, the fiends him soon inmesh!

Ah! Beauteous tripping dame with bell-like skirts,
Intent on thy small scarlet-coated hound,
Are ragged wayside babes not lovesome too?
Untrained, their state reflects on thy deserts,
Or they grow noisome beggars to abound,
Or dreaded midnight robbers breaking through.

(February 1865)

The painting depicts sturdy workmen digging up the road in Hampstead, a North London suburb, surrounded by 'the poor'. Intellectual work is represented by the two onlookers, Thomas Carlyle (with hat) and F. D Maurice, a Christian Socialist. The 'idle rich' are on horseback in the background.

Hopkins's 'Red Letter' to Bridges

I must tell you I am always thinking of the Communist future [...] I am afraid some great revolution is not far off. Horrible to say, in a manner I am a Communist [...] it is a dreadful thing for the greatest and most necessary part of a very rich nation to live a hard life without dignity, knowledge, comforts, delight, or hopes in the midst of plenty – which plenty they make. They profess that they do not care what they wreck and burn, the old civilisation and order must be destroyed. This is a dreadful look out but what has the old civilisation done for them? As it at present stands in England it is itself in great measure founded on wrecking. But they got none of the spoils, they came in for nothing but harm from it then and thereafter. England has grown hugely wealthy but this wealth has not reached the working classes; I expect it has made their condition worse. Besides this iniquitous order the old civilisation embodies another order mostly old and what is new in direct entail from the old, the old religion, learning, law, art, etc and all the history that is preserved in standing monuments. But as the working classes have not been educated they know next to nothing of all this and cannot be expected to care if they destroy it. The more I look the more black and deservedly black the future looks, so I will write no more (LB 27–8).

A Note on the Author

John Gilroy took his BA at the University of Newcastle and his MPhil at the University of Warwick. He is co-author of *A Commentary on Wordsworth's 'Prelude' 1-5* (London: Routledge and Kegan Paul, 1983) and has contributed to various literary publications. He was Senior Lecturer in English at Anglia Ruskin University, Cambridge from 1974 until 2006, and is a course director for the University of Cambridge's International Programmes.

He is also the author of *Reading Philip Larkin Selected Poems* in the Literature insights series, available from Lulu books in 9 x 6 paperback format and in a variety of Ebook formats from Google Play, Amazon Kindle, and elsewhere.

Other Literature Insights

Fields of Agony: Poetry of the First World War
English Renaissance Drama
Jane Austen, *Emma*
Joseph Conrad, *The Secret Agent*
Charles Dickens, *Bleak House*
T. S. Eliot, 'The Love Song of J. Alfred Prufrock' & *The Waste Land*
William Faulkner, *Go Down, Moses and Big Woods*
William Faulkner, *The Sound and the Fury*
Elizabeth Gaskell, *Mary Barton*
Thomas Hardy, *Selected Poems*
Thomas Hardy, *Tess of the Durbervilles*
Joseph Heller, *Catch-22*
Ted Hughes, *New Selected Poems*
Henrik Ibsen, *A Doll's House*
Philip Larkin, Selected Poems
D. H. Lawrence, *Short Sories*
D. H. Lawrence, *Sons and Lovers*
D. H. Lawrence, *Women in Love*
Toni Morrison, *Beloved*
Vladimir Nabokov, *Lolita*
William Shakespeare, *Hamlet*
William Shakespeare, *King Lear*
William Shakespeare, *Henry IV*
William Shakespeare, *Richard II*
William Shakespeare, *Richard III*
William Shakespeare, *The Merchant of Venice*
William Shakespeare, *The Tempest*
William Shakespeare, *Troilus and Cressida*
Jean Toomer, *Cane*
Mary Shelley, *Frankenstein*
William Wordsworth, *Lyrical Ballads*

www.ingramcontent.com/pod-product-compliance
Lightning Source LLC
Chambersburg PA
CBHW081339090426
42737CB00017B/3207